Forgotten Campaign:

The Story of Armstrong's Raid

Forgotten Campaign:

The Story of Armstrong's Raid

Charles Richards

Library of Congress Cataloging-in-Publication Data

ISBN: 978-1-7361525-9-1

Printed in the United States of America by Ingram Lightning Source

First edition

Cover design: Wanda Stanfill

Editing and layout: Jacque Hillman and Katie Gould

The HillHelen Group LLC
hillhelengroup@gmail.com
www.hillhelengrouppublishers.com

Table of Contents

Big Black Creek Historical Association

The monument bears witness to those who lost their lives in the Battle of Britton Lane in September 1862.

Acknowledgments

The author wishes to thank the following people and institutions for their help in providing material and direction for this book:

Wayne Moore, Tennessee State Library and Archives, Nashville, Tennessee

Jack Wood, Jackson-Madison County Public Library, Jackson, Tennessee

Dr. James Edmonson, Jackson, Tennessee

Ken Anderson, Medon, Tennessee

Dennis Suttles, Illinois State Historical Library, Springfield, Illinois

Bill Scott, Savanna, Illinois

Louise Ogg, Cairo, Illinois

Greg Koos, McLean County Historical Society, Bloomington, Illinois

Ralph Tredup, South Elgin Heritage Commission, South Elgin, Illinois

H. Scott Wolfe, Galena Public Library District, Galena, Illinois

Carolyn Autry, Indiana Historical Society, Indianapolis, Indiana

D. M. Pilcher, Mississippi Department of Archives and History, Jackson, Mississippi

John L. Ferguson, Arkansas History Commission, Little Rock, Arkansas

Drew County Historical Society, Monticello, Arkansas

Donald Holley, Monticello, Arkansas

Missouri Historical Society, St. Louis, Missouri

Coralee Paull, St. Louis, Missouri

Oklahoma Historical Society, Oklahoma City, Oklahoma

The Mary P. Shelton Public Library, Georgetown, Ohio

John Slonaker, US Army Military History Institute, Carlisle Barracks, Pennsylvania

Terrence J. Winschel, Vicksburg National Military Park, Vicksburg, Mississippi

Staff and Park Historian, Shiloh National Military Park, Shiloh, Tennessee

National Archives, Washington, DC

Preface

> "Your readers have been informed by telegraph of the recent raids of immense forces of rebel guerrillas along our whole line at different points, of their repulse, and of a skirmish having occurred between a large force of rebel cavalry, and the forces of Col. Dennis, consisting of the Twentieth and Thirtieth Illinois Infantry, a battery of artillery, and one company of Cavalry, in which the rebels were driven back; but this does not tell the tale, but leaves the impression that it was but an ordinary affair. Instead of its being a skirmish, it was one of the fiercest and most brilliant little battles yet recorded in this fearful struggle for constitutional liberty."

Thus wrote Durante Bailey, a special correspondent for the *Chicago Times*, in September 1862, about the battle of Britton's Lane, the culminating event in a military campaign known as Armstrong's Raid.

A conflict in which men give their lives for their beliefs is hard to encompass with mere words. There is still much that can be said about this short campaign. Perhaps this work will bring to light more information that has been lost to the casual historian. What we know about the sacrifice of the men of whom Mr. Bailey so eloquently spoke may become clearer with the passing of time.

This book emphasizes the men from the North and the South who rode down the dust-choked roads and died in the unharvested farm fields on a summer day more than 150 years ago. They fought and died, not in the glare of public view, but in a forgotten campaign in a remote area of the country. No camera recorded their fate and "greater" events pushed their story from the newspapers, but their sacrifice was no less than that of any other person who fought in that sectional conflict.

If their tale is improperly told, it is due to unfinished research; admittedly, the surface has hardly been scratched. But still, the purpose is to honor those men who fought the forgotten campaign.

Introduction

To understand the effect of the Civil War on West Tennessee and the role that Frank Armstrong's raid played, it is essential to take a brief look at three aspects of the social and economic development of the area prior to the war.

The first aspect to consider is the agriculture of the region and its most important crop—cotton. Second is the economic development spurred by the railroads. And third, a brief discussion of the politics and feelings of the people in the area before the war is in order.

West Tennessee is located neatly between two major rivers: the Tennessee and the Mississippi. The region's chief attraction to the early settlers was its rich farmland. Many small farmers and settlers came west across the Tennessee River to take advantage of this parcel of land opened up with its purchase from the Chickasaw Indians in 1818. But more importantly, another type of settler arrived: the slave-owning planter-farmer.

Large plantations sprang up all over the area, and their chief crop was cotton, which was ideally suited for the land and climate. It was, in fact, the main reason many men came to the region. To say that cotton was the basis of the Southern economy is almost an understatement. Cotton was the economic backbone of West Tennessee.

The world had a huge appetite for cotton, and the southern part of the United States was the main supplier of that commodity. When the Civil War broke out, many Southern politicians thought the world would demand freedom for the South rather than see their supply of cotton dwindle because of a Union naval blockade. To further the hunger for cotton worldwide, the Confederacy told its citizens to hold back their cotton from the foreign market, so cotton piled up on the plantations and rail depots with no ready markets.

Contrary to what the South had hoped, no foreign powers were willing to become involved in America's troubles to secure a supply of cotton. Instead, as the Southern economy failed, farmers and plantation owners found that the only item they had in the way of wealth was their cotton, and, to buy supplies for themselves and their families, they bartered or sold their crops to Union soldiers or Northern speculators. The effect this had on the population of the area will be discussed later, but suffice it to say that it was a bad economic decision that put the cotton on the freight platforms along the route of the Mississippi Central Railroad in the summer of 1862.

When West Tennessee was first settled, the only readily available routes of access to the area were the rivers. The Tennessee River was wild and hard to travel. The Mississippi River, in contrast, was a superhighway of sorts, heavily traveled as a primary artery of commerce. These rivers passed through West Tennessee in a north-south axis and did not reach into the hinterlands. Commerce thus depended on the tributaries of the Mississippi. These rivers—the Hatchie, Forked Deer, and Obion—ran in a general east-west direction, and most major towns of the area could be found on their banks.

In the early 1850s, the prominence of river traffic changed when a group of investors proposed building a railroad from Holly Springs, Mississippi, to Jackson, Tennessee.

To convince the people that the railroad was the wave of the future, several meetings, picnics, and barbecues were held in towns along the proposed route, where eloquent speakers led the populace to believe "that the railroad is a much safer, quicker, and cheaper conveyance than the steamboat."[1]

Anyone familiar with the rivers in the region knew that these muddy streams were wild and unpredictable, prone to flooding in the spring and nearly drying up in a hot summer. River transportation, therefore, was not always reliable. The railroads, on the other hand, ran in all sorts of weather. Every little town strove to have its own depot and freight station.

On May 12, 1858, the last rail in the construction of the Mississippi Central and Tennessee Railroad was laid near Jackson. "On that day a gaily decorated train carrying a distinguished company of guests from Holly Springs, Grand Junction, Bolivar, and other towns along the 'Grand Jackson Route,' as it was designated, whistled into Jackson and was given a noisy reception by the townspeople."[2]

The region had entered a new era. Later that same year, the Mobile and Ohio Railroad was completed between Jackson and the Kentucky border. Linked to Northern markets by rail, the whole region began to prosper from commerce.

However, when the war broke out three years later, this same artery would prove to be the highway along which the Northern armies would advance. The railroad, built with the promise of prosperity, would be fought over for the next three years, and the ruin along the line would be an example of what the whole South would eventually experience.

As war euphoria swept over the area when Tennessee seceded from the Union, many young men rushed to the Confederate cause. Yet a significant Unionist sentiment also existed in the area. At first, the pro-Union element was suppressed, but as the Union armies advanced, this feeling came more to the fore.

General Lew Wallace found this Unionist sentiment when he was stationed at Bolivar in July 1862, and, like some other Union commanders, he was served by spies and informers among the civilian populace.[3]

Slaves played their part, too. Many slave owners believed their servants were loyal, when in fact these same slaves were chief agents in tracing the movements of the Confederates. Slaves were often privy to secret information their Confederate masters discussed. The slaveholders were unaware that their bondsmen were taking careful note of what was being said.[4]

As the war entered its second year, the economy of the area suffered. Many private citizens found themselves in a tight financial fix, especially the large plantation owners. They had tons of cotton but no hard currency. To trade cotton with the Northern speculators for supplies brought down the wrath of Southern partisans who would burn their cotton and perhaps their farms. The farmers would be ruined. Yet, if they did not trade their cotton for the very essentials of life, they would find themselves slowly starving to death and going broke at the same time.

Lew Wallace, in the summer of 1862, recorded scenes of well-known planters asking the Union general for protection because they were going to "sell North." These meetings would always take place at night, for in the daylight these same planters were outstanding secessionists.[5]

Despite the bad economy and the presence of the Union army, pro-Unionist sentiment was mostly suppressed in the late summer of 1862. Yet, any setback on the battlefield was inevitably blamed on "homegrown" or "galvanized" Yankees who were spying for the North. The real bitterness that was the byproduct of the war was beginning to raise its head.

Armstrong's raid was the first of many raids that were to afflict West Tennessee. Surely it was one of the hardest-fought and most militarily thought-out ventures of the internecine fighting that would characterize the later stages of the war in the region. As the hot summer of 1862 melted into an unseasonably warm fall, the people along the line of the Mississippi Central Railroad were about to get their first taste of war and the horror it produces.

Reprint: Morningside Press, 1977

Frank Crawford Armstrong was a Federal cavalry officer turned Confederate general. He looked at the West Tennessee raid as a way to prove himself to his Confederate superiors.

Arkansas History Commission

A fire-breathing secessionist, Colonel W. F. Slemons ordered his Second Arkansas Cavalry into battle at Middleburg with the shout, 'Charge them, damn their American hearts, charge them.'

1

Armstrong Takes Command

On July 7, 1862, by special order of General Sterling Price, then commanding the Confederate Army of the West, Frank Crawford Armstrong was promoted to the rank of brigadier general.[1] This promotion made Armstrong the youngest general officer in the Confederacy, no small feat for a man who, just nine months before, was an officer in the Union army leading his men against the very cause he was now trying to preserve.[2]

Armstrong was born November 22, 1835, at the Choctaw Indian Agency, Indian Territory (now Oklahoma), where his father, a captain in the Second Dragoons, was stationed. After his father died while Frank was still a young boy, his mother remarried a general, Persifer Frazer Smith, a Mexican War hero.[3]

Frank grew to young manhood on the dusty frontier outposts of the American Southwest, and it was natural that he should follow in the footsteps of his father and stepfather and seek a military career. In 1854, he accompanied his stepfather on an expedition into New Mexico in search of marauding Apache and Navajo Indians.[4] Soon after this campaign, Armstrong went to Holy Cross Academy in

Massachusetts to round out his education. After graduating one year later, he was commissioned as a second lieutenant in the regular army and was sent back west to serve with the Second Dragoons, his father's old regiment.[5]

As a junior officer, Armstrong made a name for himself as a reliable, brave soldier. His heroism in a battle with the Comanche brought him to the attention of his commanding officer, Albert Sidney Johnston, who promoted the brave young trooper to captain.[6] Now events further to the east were to bring a dramatic change to Armstrong's life.

Prior to 1861, the Second Dragoons had been redesignated the Second Cavalry, and in the early spring of 1861, the regiment was sent to guard Washington, DC, as war fever began to sweep the country. It is unclear at this point how Armstrong felt about the coming conflict. He had seen other fellow officers leave for the South. The Second Cavalry had been home at one time or another for A. S. Johnston, Robert E. Lee, and John Bell Hood, among others. Yet, for the time being, Frank Armstrong chose duty with the Second Cavalry over any sectional loyalty.[7]

The outbreak of the war found Captain Armstrong wearing the Union blue and commanding a company of cavalry on the outskirts of Washington. In July 1861, he led his men into battle against the Confederacy at the first battle of Bull Run. The Second Cavalry's duty that day consisted mainly of fighting desperate rearguard actions against Southern cavalry after the Federal rout. Armstrong's commanding officer, Major Innis Palmer, gave command of two companies of cavalry to his energetic captain at the height of the conflict. Palmer would later state that Armstrong's "conduct . . . was in the highest degree praiseworthy."[8]

But something was happening to Armstrong, the brave Union soldier. It was, for lack of better description, a crisis of conscience, for just one month after being praised in official Union dispatches, he resigned from the Federal army in one of the most unusual events of the Civil War.

On August 13, 1861, Armstrong resigned his commission in the United States Army. Twelve other officers, some of them from the

Second Cavalry, followed suit. In a letter addressed to Secretary of War Simon Cameron, Armstrong stated in no uncertain terms that he intended to go south and fight for the Confederacy. Surprisingly, the resignation was accepted, although it broke the rules of military conduct concerning such events, and he was allowed to go unimpeded through Union lines.[9]

It is unclear why Armstrong had waited so long to change sides—long enough, in fact, to bring him into combat against an army he would later join. It has been suggested that his prewar service had brought him into contact with many important officers now leading the Confederate armies, including Johnston, Lee, and Earl Van Dorn. Perhaps he had seen a chance for advancement in his military career. The collapse of the Union army at Bull Run may have convinced Armstrong that the Federal cause was a losing one. He may have been recruited by Southern agents. All that can be said for sure is that his break with the Union had been decisive.

Free to pursue his course of action, Armstrong traveled to Arkansas to join his fortunes with the Confederacy. If he believed he would be welcomed with open arms, he was sadly disappointed, for his reception in the Southern camp was lukewarm.

A week after leaving the North, Armstrong found a position as a volunteer aide on the staff of Brigadier General Ben McCulloch. He saw no action there and later transferred to the staff of Brigadier General James M. McIntosh. At last, he had attained a rank in the Confederate army: lieutenant. There may have been some planning on Armstrong's part for this appointment since McIntosh had been in the regular army before the war and was known to Armstrong.[10]

McIntosh commanded a brigade of cavalry in the Confederate Army of the Trans-Mississippi, and Armstrong quickly became an assistant adjutant-general.[11] Yet, this new venture proved short-lived when McIntosh was killed by Union sniper fire at the battle of Pea Ridge on March 6, 1862. Armstrong was standing only a few feet away. General McCulloch also was killed that fateful day, leaving Armstrong without a superior officer to serve and without a command as well. In effect, he was unemployed.

Then followed another one of those strange events that seemed to guide Armstrong's career. The Third Louisiana Infantry elected him colonel.[12] Armstrong was surprised by the advancement but readily accepted the position. However, he would never lead these men into battle. He had only been colonel of the regiment for a little more than three months when General Sterling Price appointed him overall commander of cavalry in the newly formed Army of the West.[13] The military situation that led to Armstrong's appointment revolved around the Confederate defeat at the battle of Shiloh in April 1862.

General P. G. T. Beauregard, commanding the Confederate Army of the Mississippi, had fallen back to the vicinity of Corinth, Mississippi, with the remainder of the forces from the Shiloh battle. Meanwhile, he managed to gather additional troops from around the area until he could field a force of some 30,000 men. Even after the defeat at Pea Ridge in Arkansas, General Earl Van Dorn was able to bring to Beauregard's aid 20,000 of his own troops from across the Mississippi River. These men constituted the entire Confederate force facing the much larger Union army of General Henry Halleck, now closing in on Corinth.

Despite an overwhelming advantage in men and material, it was late May before the Union forces were ready to make their move on Corinth, and by that time Beauregard had masterminded a remarkable retreat from the town. Halleck, cautious and staid by nature, let the retreat happen under his very nose.

Faced with criticism from the government, Halleck was called back to Washington, and the Union searched for a new leader in the West. Meanwhile, things were not going smoothly in the Confederate camp. Beauregard, who had become ill after the Corinth campaign, asked General Braxton Bragg to temporarily take command of his army while he went to the Gulf coast to recuperate. But Beauregard had not notified his superiors of his plans, and when the news reached Richmond, Confederate President Jefferson Davis made the change a permanent one. Beauregard was relieved of duty, and General Braxton Bragg found himself in overall command of Confederate forces in the West.

Action in the Western Theater of the war seemed to have reached a standstill. As the Confederate forces in and around Tupelo, Mississippi, trained and rested, Southern commanders, among them General Sterling Price of Missouri, began to plan future operations. Price thought the most logical thing to do was to take his men back across the Mississippi River and retake the portion of Arkansas lost to the Federals after Pea Ridge. He felt that since the situation in Mississippi had stabilized, his troops, made up mostly of men from Arkansas and Missouri, could be spared. So convinced was Price of the need for this action that he went to Richmond to plead his case, with the full knowledge and approval of General Bragg. But instead of support he met only with rejection. For reasons not clear to Price at that time, Jefferson Davis bitterly opposed Price's plans. Dejected, Price returned to Tupelo and found that the military situation had changed since he had left.[14]

General Earl Van Dorn, Price's immediate superior, had been given command of the Confederate forces in and around Vicksburg. Bragg, meanwhile, had decided that East Tennessee, and thus the heart of the Confederacy, was threatened and he was moving the bulk of the army to its new headquarters in Chattanooga, Tennessee. This move left Price in command at Tupelo with an army of 15,000 men, many of whom were sick, and almost all of whom were poorly trained and equipped. His new command was called the Army of the West.

One of the first problems Price faced was the lack of an effective cavalry force. His army had several cavalry units, but many of these were acting as infantry. There were a few mounted units, but because of their value as scouts, they were scattered all over the countryside. Price knew these units had to be brought together in order for them to operate effectively, and he began to look for a first-class cavalry officer to whip them into shape. At General Bragg's urging, Price appointed Colonel Frank Crawford Armstrong to the post of overall commander of cavalry and made him a provisional brigadier general.[15]

The first task that Armstrong faced was getting all of those troops who called themselves cavalry mounted. Several of the Missouri and Arkansas battalions had left their mounts west of the Mississippi

River because transportation could not be found for them. Looking to private sources, Armstrong began to gather in herds of horses. The job of finding mounts for his men proved to be easier than expected since the war had not yet cut into the breeding stock.

The second task that Armstrong faced was one of organization. Few of the troops under his command had worked together in a brigade or even regimental groupings. Men such as Joseph Wheeler and Nathan Bedford Forrest had already undertaken efforts to organize the Confederate cavalry in the West, but many of Armstrong's men were still ignorant of operating together on a large scale and taking on the tasks generally assigned to cavalry.

This is where Armstrong's years as a professional soldier came into play. He immediately began to gather all the scattered units in his area of command and set about drilling them relentlessly. His men came to know him as a fair, but tough, drillmaster. Soldiers knew better than to incur his wrath, and those unfortunate enough to cross him were cursed and subjected to all sorts of humiliation. Armstrong became noted for the abusive language he would heap on errant soldiers.[16]

The Confederates' quiet respite before Tupelo gave Armstrong the time he needed to accomplish his intense training program. His cavalrymen learned to fight, mounted or dismounted. He encouraged the use of the saber, the traditional cavalry weapon. Some of his men who had felt themselves inadequate for any task just weeks before took well to the strict training and became "ready and eager to measure arms with the Federal cavalry."[17]

These troops formed the core of what came to be known as Armstrong's Brigade. They were a mixed collection of men, many with little or no combat experience, but all now willing to prove themselves in battle.

His brigade included the Second Arkansas Cavalry under the command of opinionated, quick-tempered Colonel William F. Slemons. Slemons was born March 15, 1830, in Weakley County, Tennessee, where he spent most of his early childhood. He received his higher education at Bethel Seminary in Carroll County, where he studied to be a schoolteacher. When Slemons's family moved to Arkansas in 1853, he followed and taught school for a while, but he quickly became restless. Late in the fall of 1853, he moved back to Tennessee and began to study law at Cumberland University, where he graduated in 1854.[18]

After returning to Arkansas, Slemons was admitted to the bar and set up practice near the family home at Monticello. Because of his interest in politics, he found himself elected and serving in the state Senate during the fateful year of 1861. Slemons was an avid states rightist who later would glory in the role he played in leading Arkansas out of the Union.[19]

When the war broke out, he joined the Confederate army as a private. Displeased with the actions of the colonel of the cavalry battalion in which he was enlisted, Slemons challenged the man to a duel. When the colonel refused, word got around that he was a coward and Slemons was elected the battalion's new colonel. As colonel, he commanded a new regiment, the Second Arkansas Cavalry. Some of the men in the regiment were veteran troops and some were green, but Slemons promised that with these men he would "do something for my bleeding country." Largely ill-equipped, the Arkansas men were, at least in morale, ready to go to war.[20]

Another regiment in Armstrong's Brigade was the Second Missouri Cavalry, led by the "austere old colonel" Robert "Black Bob" McCulloch.

McCulloch was forty-two years old when his men were brigaded under Armstrong. An old-school soldier, McCulloch assumed a quiet, dignified, yet commanding presence. A biographer would note, "Col. McCulloch, although a man of strong personality and a strict disciplinarian, was as gentle and tender as a woman. He knew personally every man in his regiment, and when in camp made their comfort his first consideration; but he would lead them with fierce and reckless daring into the very thickest of the fray."

A firm believer in the use of the saber, McCulloch had drilled his men relentlessly for months on the art of mounted warfare. He had commanded Missouri state troops early in the war at Pea Ridge and

Wilson's Creek, and it was not until the first part of August 1862 that his regiment was "confederated."[21]

McCulloch's men presented a contrast to their Arkansas neighbors. The Second Missouri was well-armed and well-equipped, as the secessionists in that state had made sure these men were not only armed with the newest breech-loading carbines, but with pistols and sabers as well. After months of training, they felt they had no equals in the use of the saber, and they were considered by many to be the best-trained cavalry in the Army of the West.[22]

Another part of Armstrong's growing command was Wirt Adams's Cavalry Battalion. Adams was a successful banker and planter who had served the Army of the Republic of Texas in 1839. As a member of the Mississippi state legislature in 1858 and 1860, he had been an outspoken and ardent supporter of secession. For Adams's service in leading Mississippi out of the Union, Jefferson Davis offered him the position of postmaster general of the Confederacy. Adams, however, declined the offer and opted to lead troops in the field. To this end, he raised a battalion of cavalry and was made its colonel. Adams had sought to have his command designated the First Mississippi Cavalry, but when he found out that another unit had already been so named, he named his unit after himself, declining to call his battalion the Second Mississippi Cavalry.[23]

Wirt Adams's Cavalry Battalion was made up of a collection of independent units from Alabama, Mississippi, and Louisiana. The Louisiana troops, in fact, were a "gift" to Adams from the governor of that state due to Adams's popularity and political pull. However, taken together as a unit, the battalion was small and rather ill-equipped, being armed mainly with sabers, pistols, and double-barreled shotguns. The battalion had been only lightly engaged in the opening stages of the war, being used primarily for scouting and raiding. Early in August of 1861, it was brought under Armstrong's command.[24]

As the summer of 1862 progressed, Armstrong's Brigade grew by one more regiment, the Second Tennessee Cavalry under the command of Colonel C. R. Barteau. Barteau was a native of Ohio who had become convinced of the rightness of the Southern cause. A schoolteacher by profession, he had moved to Tennessee before the war to edit a pro-secession newspaper. After the war broke out, he joined the Confederate cavalry, where his reputation as a strict disciplinarian helped him rise quickly through the ranks.[25]

The men of the Second Tennessee Cavalry came mostly from West Tennessee, with a good number of Mississippi troops thrown in for good measure. Two months after it had been formed, the regiment was taken into Armstrong's Brigade. The unit had a dubious reputation, however, for it had been organized and reorganized so often that its own officers later stated that at that point it was "almost totally devoid of discipline." So harsh was its reputation that the regiment had only been used for picket duty and light scouting.[26]

As the training of these men progressed and their proficiency increased, Armstrong began to consider the possibility of using them in a large-scale operation. Early in July 1862, he presented a number of suggestions in an informal manner to his superior, General Price. Then late that same month, an event took place that was to play a pivotal role in Armstrong's future plans and operations.

During the last week of July, General Joseph Wheeler, commanding the cavalry in Bragg's newly organized Army of the Tennessee, led a raid behind Union lines into West Tennessee. The objective was to screen the movement of Bragg's army from the Tupelo area to its new headquarters in Chattanooga. In some respects, the raid miscarried. Wheeler started out with a thousand men from Holly Springs, Mississippi, and marched toward Tennessee, but before he could reach the state line, his force had been reduced to approximately five hundred men due to the demand for mounted patrols elsewhere on the front. However, he was able to raid up the line of the Mississippi Central Railroad as far as Middleburg, Tennessee.

Wheeler accomplished little. He burned some cotton and destroyed a few trestles before retreating to Mississippi before a superior force of Union cavalry. Although the raid was of minor military importance, it had a far-reaching effect on the strategic thinking of commanders both North and South.

The idea was planted in the minds of some men in the Confederate high command that a large-scale raid along the same lines could accomplish much in the way of disrupting the Union war effort. A major supply route, the Mississippi Central Railroad, was poorly guarded at that time. They reasoned that a raid of larger purpose and with greater numbers could surely accomplish much in West Tennessee.

Prior to Wheeler's raid, Armstrong had taken his new brigade on its first campaign as a united cavalry force. On July 17, Armstrong was ordered, under Special Order 123, to advance on Decatur, Alabama, and the Tennessee River and "operate at its own direction, doing all practicable things to harass the enemy and cut off any detachments or supply trains."[27]

This raid conceived to harass the growing Union forces in the Shiloh-Corinth area was a test by fire of Armstrong's leadership. He jumped at the chance, carefully planning each move and spending days and nights plotting and patrolling his route of march. He led an assortment of troops, including some hastily gathered to his command, but McCulloch's Second Missouri and Barteau's Second Tennessee formed the backbone of this group. Still, in all, he had only 651 men.[28]

Considering a strong pro-Union sentiment in the part of Alabama through which he had to march, Armstrong took an indirect route toward his goal and met with unqualified success. A participant in that raid, R. R. Hancock of the Second Tennessee Cavalry, gave this account of the campaign:

> "General Armstrong's Brigade—composed of Colonels McCulloch's and Kelly's Battalions, a Louisiana squadron, and two companies commanded by Hill and Saunders—passing Bay Springs on the 18th of July, was then and there joined by Colonel Barteau with four companies of his regiment—in all about seven hundred troopers.
>
> Marching east four days, Armstrong arrived at Moulton, in North Alabama; thence by a forced march to Courtland, he surprised and routed a Federal force—two companies of infantry

and one of cavalry—encamped at that place, capturing one hundred and thirty two. He also captured ten wagons, about fifty mules and ten good horses, three hundred bushels of corn, some oats, a good lot of ammunition, commissaries enough for seven days' rations, including several sacks of coffee and salt, and a lot of small arms. Four of the Federals were wounded; the number killed unknown. Colonel Kelly, in a skirmish below Courtland, killed about twelve Federals; wounded unknown. Colonel Kelly returned to Moulton with a few prisoners. The Federal loss in this expedition—killed, wounded, and prisoner—was 194.

After falling back to Moulton, General Armstrong paroled the prisoners. A few days after this he started back to North Mississippi, and on the 10th of August he returned to and encamped along the Mobile and Ohio Railroad, near Guntown."[29]

General Armstrong's success had not only brought him a measure of confidence in his own ability to lead, but it showed his fledgling brigade he could fight. Armstrong also gained the respect of his superiors. In a dispatch dated August 3, General Bragg noted: "Convey to General Armstrong my cordial congatulations [sic] at his successes. The conduct of himself and his gallant command shall be made the subject of a special dispatch to the Government."[30]

Armstrong's victories came at a time when the Confederate government was in dire need of good news. Armstrong knew that his mention in official dispatches would confirm his position as brigadier general, a rank that the Confederate Congress had yet to formally approve. In the summer of 1862, Confederate hopes were riding high. Victory for the Southern Confederacy seemed within easy grasp, but to secure final victory, one thing was most desired, and in fact needed, by the South, and that was the recognition of a foreign power, preferably Great Britain or France. Foreign recognition would mean that the Confederacy would be accepted in the "family of nations."

Southern leadership knew that to accomplish this they needed to achieve more on the battlefield and to show, once and for all, that they were not about to be subdued by the might of the North. The South had to show that its armies were not only able to hold ground but to wage offensive warfare as well.

Two states seemed to the Confederates likely prospects for "liberation," that is to say, theaters for offensive warfare. These were the border states of Maryland and Kentucky. Both states had furnished soldiers to the Southern cause and were thought to have a large majority of Confederate sympathizers who were being "held down" by Union armies. Thus, it was to the "liberation" of Maryland and Kentucky that the Confederates turned their attention.

In the east, General Robert E. Lee was making plans to move his army into Maryland, and in Chattanooga, General Braxton Bragg planned an invasion of Kentucky. Success by either, or both, would be the anticipated boost needed to gain foreign support. But even with all of the coordinated planning of these men, they faced a growing problem: a lack of manpower.

The Union forces in the West were almost three times larger than the Confederate armies. In Chattanooga, General Bragg learned that some Union troops had already marched into Kentucky in anticipation of his planned invasion there. To even the odds in Kentucky, Bragg wanted General Price's Army of the West, at Tupelo, to tie down as many Union troops in North Mississippi and West Tennessee as possible. Bragg tried to convince Price that his intelligence proved West Tennessee was ripe for invasion. He believed that by invading West Tennessee, Price would keep Union forces under U. S. Grant from sending reinforcements to Kentucky to oppose Confederate operations.

General Bragg urged Price to invade Tennessee in early August, but Price, with only 15,000 men at Tupelo, saw the foolishness of such a move. Price knew that to get to Tennessee he would have to pass a large Federal army, twice the size of his own, at Corinth. Besides, the Union army at Corinth was well entrenched and probably awaiting orders to march southward. Much seemed to ride on Price's ability to tie down the forces on his front, but the possibility of doing so was slim.

General Price was no quitter or shirker of duty, so under Bragg's urging, he began to consider other options. He finally concluded that although he could not commit his entire army to a strike northward, he could, and would, commit his cavalry.[31]

Two considerations figured heavily in Price's decision for a cavalry raid to Tennessee. First, General Joe Wheeler's ride to Middleburg in mid-July had demonstrated how disruptive such an action could be on the fragile Union rail communications. Second, Price had already been impressed by the progress his mounted troops had made in training under General Armstrong. Armstrong seemed a capable leader, and his brigade had been tested in the raid into Alabama. They were ready, Price felt, to take on a larger, more important task.

Armstrong jumped at the chance of leading his men in an independent campaign. Ever since Wheeler's July raid, Armstrong had hoped for such an opportunity. He was firmly convinced such a venture could reap great benefits and here, at last, was a chance to prove it. Generals Price and Armstrong began to discuss the plan for the raid and quickly decided on some guidelines. Price was confident enough in Armstrong's ability to give him leeway in planning the operation of the campaign. It was decided that whereas Price would designate the troops to be used, Armstrong would be left with the final planning and execution of the campaign.

It was probably at this early date that a misunderstanding occurred between the commanders. Just what Price truly expected of Armstrong is unclear. What is clear, however, is that the overall intent of the campaign was becoming clouded. The various officers involved, as they began to speak of the coming campaign, described it in very different terms. Price called the planned operation a reconnaissance, while Armstrong referred to it as a raid, and Bragg called the effort a diversionary tactic. Each man was developing his own purpose.

Price and Armstrong both had much at stake in the venture, not only in hoped-for results but also in energy and manpower. Price was willing to commit almost all of his cavalry to the operation. Armstrong was more than ready to lead them since there was a sense of prestige to the campaign, as it would be the first large-scale cavalry raid by the Confederates in the Western Theater.

Word began to filter down through the ranks in mid-August that something big was about to happen. Armstrong's Brigade began an intensive training program. R. R. Hancock, a private in the Second Tennessee Cavalry, recorded these changes in his diary. On August 15, 1862, he wrote: "An order was read at dress parade requiring us to drill on horseback in the morning, foot in the evening, go on a dress parade once a day, and prepare as fast as possible for a more vigorous campaign."[32]

By August 17, the plans were more fully known. Hancock noted: "General Armstrong was making preparations for an expedition into West Tennessee . . ."[33]

On that date, the cavalry regiments under Armstrong's command were ordered to prepare ten days' rations and to march with only one wagon for every two companies.[34] The coming campaign was to be one of lightning moves, and the regiments were ordered to trim down to a lean fighting shape. At this point, Armstrong's forces consisted of the Second Arkansas Cavalry, under Colonel W. F. Slemons; the Second Tennessee Cavalry, commanded by Colonel C. R. Barteau; Wirt Adams's Cavalry Battalion, led by Colonel Wirt Adams himself; and one battalion of the Third Tennessee Cavalry, under the command of Major Charles Balch.

The addition of Major Balch's men to Armstrong's growing forces was a fluke. These Tennessee troops had been detached from the Third Regiment for scouting duties. Somehow, this independent battalion became attached to the Second Tennessee Cavalry, although Major Balch insisted they were a separate command. Independent or not, they were earmarked for participation in the raid. This was to be a homecoming for these men since many of them were from West Tennessee.[35]

The Second Missouri Cavalry, a regiment originally in Armstrong's Brigade, was now attached to another independent cavalry brigade under the command of Colonel William H. Jackson. Word had passed through the ranks, however, that these men were soon to rejoin the brigade. Marching by a circuitous route, Armstrong's Brigade reached the Tallahatchie River, just south of Holly Springs, Mississippi, on the night of August 25.[36] It was here that Armstrong had arranged to meet with Jackson's men.

Jackson was the acting colonel of the Seventh Tennessee Cavalry, having taken command from Nathan Bedford Forrest after Forrest was wounded at Shiloh. Colonel Jackson had graduated thirty-eighth in a class of forty-nine at West Point in 1856. He served in the US Cavalry and fought against the Indians in New Mexico and Kansas. When war clouds began to gather in the east, however, he was faced with a dilemma, because although he was personally opposed to the idea of war, he believed in the Southern cause. So rather than fight against his home state, Jackson resigned his commission in the US Army and joined the Confederacy. A hulking, barrel-chested figure, Jackson was a strict, by-the-book soldier whose experience and knowledge made him a valuable officer.[37]

Jackson's regiment, the Seventh Tennessee Cavalry, was formed of men from the western part of the state who were veteran troops, more so than most men under Armstrong's immediate command. Bloodied at Shiloh and participants in several small raids and skirmishes, the Seventh Tennessee was already a lean fighting unit. These men, like most of the rest of the Western Cavalry, were armed with pistols, sabers, and double-barreled shotguns.

Also under Jackson's command was the First Mississippi Cavalry under the leadership of Colonel Richard Alexander Pinson. Born in Lincoln County, Tennessee, Pinson had moved at an early age to Mississippi, where his family had established the town of Pontotoc. With a background of education and influence, Pinson used his political leverage to guide Mississippi out of the Union. He joined the Confederate army as a private in 1861, but by mid-summer of 1862, he was the colonel of the First Mississippi Cavalry. Tall, handsome, and powerfully built, Pinson was beloved by his men.[38]

Pinson's troopers, like the men of the Seventh Tennessee, were battle-seasoned veterans. Raised mainly in North Mississippi, his men were armed with breech-loading Maynard carbines and had fought as an organized unit at Belmont, Missouri; Shiloh, Tennessee; and Corinth, Mississippi.[39]

General Price ordered these men to unite with Armstrong's Brigade at Holly Springs, where Jackson was to turn over command of his brigade to Armstrong. Just how Jackson felt about this change of command is unrecorded. A problem that had faced the Confederate high command during the early planning stages of the united cavalry force in the Army of the West was one of command. Surely Jackson had been considered for overall command, but at an early date Armstrong had won out, perhaps because he claimed Arkansas as his home, which set well with the troops from the Trans-Mississippi Theater. Armstrong was helped, no doubt, by the promotion of his abilities to General Price by Braxton Bragg.

The special order that made Armstrong a brigadier general also gave him control over "all regiments, battalions, unattached companies, and squads of cavalry in the Army of the West."[40] By this authority, Armstrong was able to take into his command not only Jackson's brigade but the lone battalion of the Third Tennessee Cavalry as well.

It was Tuesday, August 26, when just before daylight, Armstrong moved his men into Holly Springs and formed them in a dress parade down the main street. At precisely nine o'clock, Jackson's men rode into town.[41] This juncture of Armstrong's and Jackson's forces made up the largest cavalry force ever assembled by the Confederates in the Western Theater of the war for any single purpose. Having finally collected his men together, Armstrong marched them at a slow pace toward Grand Junction, Tennessee, the jumping-off point for the raid. In all, he mustered just over 2,700 men.

Now, however, Armstrong began to dawdle. He advanced toward Tennessee at a leisurely pace, and some men in Jackson's brigade fretted at first that the campaign had somehow miscarried. An officer recorded, "The boys became impatient for fear of being disappointed. Having ascertained the previous night that they would leave the next morning, they became vocifforous [sic] with shouts of exultion [sic]. None were sad but those that could not go."[42]

Armstrong resolved to carry on, and the next day in a dispatch, General Price notified General Earl Van Dorn, at Vicksburg, of Armstrong's campaign: "I have sent General Frank C. Armstrong, with almost 2,000 cavalry, upon an intended reconnaissance. He will make a circuit of Corinth, striking at whatever points may appear most available."[43]

But Armstrong appeared to have thought more of his raid than just a reconnaissance. Although at this point the Confederates seemed to have been planning a strike at Corinth, which indeed would happen a month later, General Armstrong wanted to do far more than gather information on the Union army at Corinth. Instead, in a letter dated the same day as Price's dispatch to Van Dorn, he told his commander of his goals for the first time.

"I shall move with my command and about 1,100 men, under Colonel Jackson, threaten Bolivar, and, if possible, take Jackson and destroy the Mobile and Ohio Railroad," Armstrong wrote.[44]

Thus, his grand design was to raid far into the rear of the Union army. He did not seem content to accomplish the objective set by General Price of a reconnaissance around the Federal army in North Mississippi. Instead, Armstrong was bent upon going fifty miles in the opposite direction toward Jackson, Tennessee. His superiors accepted the news that Jackson was his goal, even though the news must have been a shock to Price.

Armstrong's two brigades reached LaGrange, Tennessee, on the evening of August 27. It had been a wonderful, eventful day for the Confederate troopers. Their appearance in West Tennessee had been a heartening experience for the civilian populace. One officer noted, "Along the road (where we marched) the ladies were greeting us and singing patriotic songs."[45]

And there were other incidents of greeting and outpourings of friendship. A Mr. Smith was well remembered by the troops under Armstrong: "This Mr. Smith was a 'whole soul reb,' as the following will plainly show. Our forage master asked him if we could get something from him to feed our horses. His answer was, 'Do not ask me such a question.' Using his index finger, 'There is my corn field, there is my corn crib, and there is my smoke house; just help yourself.' "[46]

Armstrong and his men feasted on the hospitality of their host and rested, now safely in Tennessee. General Armstrong's strategy had been based on some sound principles. He had come to Tennessee to disrupt Federal supplies and communications. His objectives lay along the Mississippi Central Railroad that cut through the heart of West Tennessee. He had gathered together the largest cavalry force in the Western Theater for that purpose. His goals and how they were to be achieved were clearly set, at least in his own mind, and now having crossed an undefined "no man's land," he was set to accomplish his tasks. His two biggest assets were his troops' familiarity with the area and the tactical element of surprise. To the end of accomplishing complete surprise, Armstrong planned an indirect approach to his objectives, as he had done a month before on the Courtland, Alabama, raid, but unknown to him, his tactical advantage had already begun to slip away.

Library of Congress

On July 7, 1862, General Sterling Price (above), then commanding the Confederate Army of the West, promoted Frank Crawford Armstrong to the rank of brigadier general.

US Army Military History Institute

Colonel Michael Lawler (above), post commander of Jackson, was charged by General Ross to organize a defense of that city. His orders brought on the Battle of Britton's Lane.

2

'A Patent Way of Making War'

When General Halleck was called back to Washington after he bungled the Corinth campaign, the Union forces in the Western Theater faced the major task of reorganization.

In July 1862, Halleck turned over his command to General Ulysses S. Grant, making Grant the overall commander of all Union forces west of the Tennessee River. Grant divided this huge area into four smaller, more manageable districts: the District of Memphis, the District of Corinth, the District of Cairo, and the District of West Tennessee. The District of West Tennessee stretched from the Mississippi state line north to Western Kentucky and from the District of Memphis east to the Tennessee River. Thus, the district took in the towns of Brownsville, Somerville, Bolivar, Purdy, Grand Junction, and Jackson.

West Tennessee was no longer an area of major conflict in the war, and the Union army set about the task of garrison and occupation duty. Yet, there was a cloud on the horizon.

The Confederate cavalry raid into West Tennessee late in July 1862 awakened dread in the Union commanders overseeing operations there. The raid exposed a problem that had plagued military men for years. That difficulty was one of maintaining long supply lines through territory that was strong in enemy sentiment. Union generals felt they had been lucky in warding off Confederate attacks on their supply lines, but in war, nothing can be left to chance or luck.

Union advances into the heartland of the South were often made along the lines of rivers and railroads. In this way, the advancing armies had a line of supply in their rear. But these lines, at least as far as the railroads were concerned, could be tenuous. Union commanders sought ways to protect their rail lines at all costs. By August 1862, a system of garrisons and mounted patrols was put into place.

Each town that had a railroad depot would have a garrison of infantry. An infantry guard was to be placed at each major bridge and trestle along the line. Between each infantry garrison there was to be a constant mounted patrol of cavalry. It was this system that General John McClernand, overall commander in the District of West Tennessee, began to set up between Grand Junction and Jackson along the forty-mile line of the Mississippi Central railway.

Grand Junction, close to the Mississippi state line, was judged to be too close to enemy territory to be effectively garrisoned. Any force at Grand Junction would have to be large, and it was thought that this would only attract unwanted Confederate attention. Thus, Union cavalry dispatched from Bolivar patrolled the town on a weekly basis.

The idea that a large force close to the Mississippi state line might invite a Confederate attack underlined a fear among Northern generals at this stage in the war. A Southern attack into West Tennessee, it was thought, could develop into a full-blown invasion, and such an invasion, no matter how small, would have meant that the Shiloh campaign was for naught. If the Confederates once again came to occupy West Tennessee, it would set the Union war effort back by months. This fear of a Confederate attack was to shade military operations in the region throughout the summer and fall of 1862.[1]

The next town up the line from Grand Junction was Middleburg, a small farming community and rail stop five miles south of Bolivar.

Because the town was so close to the large Union garrison in Bolivar, it did not have a garrison of its own, but cavalry patrolled it daily.

Bolivar, the Hardeman County seat, was the headquarters of the Second Division of McClernand's corps. Seven thousand Union soldiers were camped there, including infantry, artillery, and cavalry. The town was heavily fortified because it was the largest Union garrison south of the Hatchie River and relatively close to the Mississippi state line.

The commander at Bolivar was an Illinoisan named Leonard Fulton Ross. Brigadier General Ross was dynamic, young, ambitious, and bored with his garrison duty. Everything south of Bolivar was under his jurisdiction. But by August, Ross was growing weary of his duty and asked for a leave to go home; his request, for the time being, was denied.[2]

Next up the rail line from Bolivar, after crossing the Hatchie River north of town, was the station at Toone, a quiet little town in an area of gently rolling land that presented the illusion of being located in some mountainous foothills. Toone was garrisoned by five companies of the Forty-Fifth Illinois Infantry under the command of Colonel Jasper Maltby.

Maltby, like his superior, Ross, was young and ambitious but disillusioned by garrison life. He led the Forty-Fifth Illinois Infantry, also known as the "Washburn Lead Mine Regiment." The men of the Forty-Fifth Illinois had the reputation of being a fighting unit "par excellence." Always in the thick of battle, they had lost 47 percent of their men at the battle of Shiloh. The garrison duty along the railroad was meant to be a rest period for these men.[3] In fact, they had been personally ordered to this post by General McClernand, their corps commander.[4]

However, there was also a more practical reason behind this move. Pro-Union home guard units stationed in the area had been unable to keep Confederate "rangers" from burning trestles and bridges and causing general havoc along the line. It was decided that what was needed were veteran professional troops on guard.

North of Toone was Teague, a small whistle stop on the rail line without a proper depot. A water tower and wood yard to service the trains were located about a mile north of town on the banks of Clover Creek. Locals called this stop the "wood yard," but the Union troops stationed there, Company C of the Forty-Fifth Illinois Infantry, called the place Treadger Station. A long trestle across the creek at Treadger made the place more valuable from a strategic point of view than the nearby town of Teague. It was for this reason Teague was never garrisoned.

Ten miles farther north was Medon Station, a growing town of churches, stores, and schools. Here the Forty-Fifth Illinois had stationed the remainder of its men. This garrison's main concern was guarding the small trestle just south of town.

The next stop up the line was Jackson, the Madison County seat, and with several thousand residents, it was by far the largest town on the line. Colonel Michael Lawler was the garrison commander. Lawler oversaw a town considered so far in the Union rear that it was but lightly garrisoned. It served mainly as a supply depot, hospital, and rest area for the Union forces. Hundreds of sick and wounded soldiers were billeted in the town. The city did serve one other important function; it was the headquarters for the military District of West Tennessee, no doubt chosen because of its central location geographically in the district. The city also was a staging area for new troops being sent to the front lines farther south. Here, too, veteran regiments, much decreased in manpower by heavy fighting, were assigned to recuperate from their losses.

Not only was the protection of the railroads important to the Union forces in West Tennessee, but so was the security of the rivers in the region. Of primary importance was the Hatchie River, which cut West Tennessee in half from east to west. The river was muddy and wild, although it was navigable most of the year. It had been used for commerce in the early history of the region but had long since lost its prominence in that area due to the advent of the railroad. The railroads crossed the river in various places by bridges and trestles, but the many fords and ferries that connected roads on the opposite sides created a bigger problem for the Union military planners. The single most important ford was one at the tiny settlement of Estanaula in Madison County.

Estanaula is a Cherokee Indian phrase that roughly translates as "here we can cross." Because the bank sloped well there and the water was shallow for most of the year, there had always been a ford at this point in the river. Since the 1830s, a major stage road had run through this point between Jackson and Bolivar. But when people spoke of the crossing at Estanaula, they could have been referring to any of three fords on the river close to that town.

First, there was the much-used ford, and later ferry, at the Steam Mill Ferry crossing. Named for a nearby steam-operated grist mill, this ford was also called the Memphis ford because the stage road that ran through there made connections to that town.

Second was the main ford at the town of Estanaula itself. A ferry had been placed there, too, but wading was still the preferred way to cross.

The third and final ford was known as the lower ford or the Somerville crossing. The road that made its way across the river there connected with the county seat in Fayette County, Tennessee.

If indeed, at a later date, Confederate troops did march into West Tennessee, then the Hatchie River could act as a natural defensive line behind which a Union army could gather strength to make a stand. But the Hatchie also presented the unique problem of being crisscrossed with a great number of bridges, ferries, and fords that all had to be guarded and watched. After the Confederate raid of late July 1862, it was decided that these places, along with the railroads, must be guarded.

To that end, the post commander at Jackson, Colonel Michael Lawler, chose two depleted regiments of veteran infantry to guard the Estanaula fords. He assigned the Twentieth and Thirtieth Illinois Infantry regiments, under the command of Colonel Elias Dennis, to the task.

Both the Twentieth and Thirtieth Illinois had suffered much over the previous year of hard campaigning. The units had been brigaded together early in the war and had fought at Belmont, Fort Donelson, and Shiloh, where they had been in the thick of the fighting. Together, the regiments could field no more than 600 effective men, but giving Colonel Dennis this assignment was considered a wise move. Educated and observant, he was making a name for himself as a capable field officer.[5]

During the second week of August, Dennis marched his battle-tried veterans to Estanaula and set up camp. Quickly, he began to note the deficiencies of his force to the task assigned.

Within a week of his arrival at Estanaula, Dennis was reinforced by a two-gun section of artillery from Battery E, Second Illinois Artillery. This unit, too, had been whittled away by the war. First known as Schwartz's battery and later as Gumbart's, the two-gun section, due to officer promotion and battle casualties, was now commanded by 2nd Lieutenant William Dengel.[6] Several of the battery's guns had been captured by the Confederates at Shiloh, and the two six-pounder field pieces were all the battery had serviceable.[7]

Two problems stymied Union plans concerning the Hatchie River defenses. The first was one of manpower. There were too few troops to properly guard all the crossings along the river. More men were badly needed, and those needed most were cavalry. The second problem was one of weather. West Tennessee was in the throes of a terrible drought. The level of the Hatchie River was falling rapidly, and the stream was losing its effectiveness as a barrier.

Studying the situation from a distant perspective, the Union high command set about to solve these problems. Writing from his headquarters in Memphis, General Grant, in a dispatch dated August 9, ordered all bridges or ferries across the Hatchie that were not essential to Union supply movements burned or otherwise destroyed so that the Union troops would have fewer places to patrol.[8] This immediately caused confusion among the local commanders because they were unsure who had the authority to destroy these bridges. Besides, with the river level falling because of the drought, it was becoming apparent that the Hatchie could be crossed at many new places. The idea of the Hatchie River as a possible defensive line was diminishing.

The question of manpower was easier to solve. On August 15, Dennis got some relief at Estanaula when the Fourth Ohio Independent Cavalry Company arrived under the command of Captain Charles Foster.

The Fourth Ohio Cavalry had been General Halleck's personal bodyguard when he commanded the Union army at Corinth some months before but was left behind when he was called back to Washington. Numbering a few more than a hundred men, they had been sent to Dennis.[9] These men were well trained, well equipped, and well led, but there was a drawback to their presence.

Lack of geographical knowledge concerning the area hindered the Union commanders in their planning. The Union army was almost totally ignorant of the road systems, the courses of creeks and rivers, or the lay of the land. Having advanced through this part of West Tennessee along the lines of the railroads or along the larger Tennessee River, they were hard-pressed to find their way around the swampy lands bordering the Hatchie. Colonel Dennis had recognized this problem from the onset of his stay at Estanaula and tried to remedy it.

On August 16, Dennis wrote to General McClernand in Jackson requesting that a cavalry officer identified as Captain Curtis, who knew the area around Estanaula, be assigned to his command.

Dennis stated his case succinctly: "Acquainted with all roads, paths, and country generally—I am satisfied he would be of more service to the country than double the number of men wholly unacquainted."[10]

This veiled reference to the near uselessness of the Fourth Ohio Cavalry, due to their lack of knowledge of the area, went unheeded by McClernand, so Dennis took matters into his own hands. He directed an artillery officer, Lieutenant Emil Steger, to accompany patrols along the Hatchie River in the Estanaula area. From these patrols, Steger, to the best of his ability, drew a map containing notations of houses, farms, fields, roads, and Union troop positions. Even though the map was not to scale, Dennis was pleased enough with the effort to send a copy to McClernand himself. At least now Dennis and his fellow officers had some idea of the lay of the land.[11]

Then on August 19, Dennis sent a report on the situation at Estanaula that contained some rather prophetic statements. Patrolling through the Hatchie River bottom along land that should have been swampy, Dennis was shocked to find that the drought had baked the ground brick dry. And there was another revelation. A place eight miles east of Estanaula, where Clover Creek merged into the Hatchie, was now fordable.

Dennis noted: "I found the ford at the mouth of Clover Creek not more than three feet deep and can easily be forded by cavalry, and I believe artillery and trains. . . ."[12]

Dennis began to feel that he was faced with an impossible mission. He set about building a series of blockhouses along the Hatchie at the principal fords, but he left the bulk of his forces just above Estanaula.

Dennis was reinforced again a few days later by forty-three men of Company H, Twelfth Illinois Cavalry. These men, under the command of Captain Franklin Gilbert, were green and untried. With their carbines[13] and blue coats, their only pieces of "regulation" uniform, these men were trying to fit into the role assigned to them. Like the Fourth Ohio Cavalry, they had to rely on the Steger map to mount a patrol.

So it was with these commands that the Union army awaited the discretion of the Confederates. The lull before the storm was enjoyed by those units too long at the front and so far from home. The regimental historian of the Forty-Fifth Illinois Infantry wrote of those days while stationed at Medon:

> "Thus stationed we enjoyed a quiet easy camp life, with not much else to do but eat 'peach cobblers' (you remember them, don't you boys?) chickens, geese, &c., which somehow or other would find their way into camp, although there were strict orders against foraging. You know at the time it was the custom for our army to guard rebel property, return to their masters runaway slaves, and all that kind of thing, a kind of patent way the government had of making war tender and merciful."[14]

It was into this peaceful scene that Armstrong's raiders were about to make their appearance. Armstrong's two brigades reached LaGrange, Tennessee, on the evening of August 27 and rested there for a full day. Union patrols had been seen in the area the day before, but it seemed, at least for the moment, that the Confederate movements were unknown to the Federals.

However, Armstrong's arrival was not a secret. General Grant had sent a dispatch to Colonel Marcellus Crocker in Bolivar on August 26, stating he had information that 6,000 Confederate cavalrymen were fast approaching the area and "had been sent to attack our lines."[15]

Even though Armstrong's intentions of striking into West Tennessee were known to the Union high command, his numbers had been greatly overestimated, and this was to greatly affect Union battle plans over the next few days. Thinking that the Confederates intended to "invade" West Tennessee, the Union generals had convinced themselves that Armstrong's men were the advance guard of a larger force.

For his part, Armstrong never intimated to anyone that he was an advance guard. He presented himself solely as the leader of a large raiding party, one that, in fact, made up a third of all the Confederate cavalry in Mississippi.

Unknown to Armstrong, his movement across the state line into Tennessee had been detected. His presence was observed by slaves and loyal Union farmers who were doing their best to spread the word of Armstrong's approach. One officer who had his own personal and "perfectly reliable"[16] source of information was Colonel Dennis at Estanaula. Dennis had the service of a pro-Union civilian who seemed to have been privy to much information about the Confederates. Dennis often spoke of him in reports and dispatches but never by name.

By August 29, Dennis knew that Armstrong's force did not number much more than 2,000 men, not the 6,000 spoken of in Grant's dispatch.[17] And he knew that this force was not part of a major Confederate offensive to retake West Tennessee.

Dennis's men had been on a heightened state of alert for about a week before Armstrong appeared in LaGrange. Granville McDonald, the Thirtieth Illinois regimental historian, recorded an incident at Estanaula that illustrates this tension.

> "We had quite a scare one night, some darkeys were trying to cross the river and come into our camp. The pickets fired on them and broke a horse's leg, and he got down in the water and made such a noise, the pickets kept up firing awhile. The drum major was ordered to beat the long roll. He got out in his shirt tail, and it being a still night, it would have almost raised the dead to hear that drum through the beech trees. The boys were soon in line, some dressed, some half dressed, and some not dressed at all, but all had their fighting traps on ready to lick any number of Johnnies. But when the facts were known, some laughed, some swore about having such an excitment [sic], and spoiling their nap, about an old horse down in the river with a broken leg."[18]

The men of Dennis's force had a good laugh over the incident, but the next time the drums beat the long roll at night, it would be deadly serious.

US Army Military History Institute

Commanding a mixed brigade, Colonel Elias Dennis marched to relieve the surrounded garrison at Medon. Instead, on a little-used farm road called Britton's Lane, he ran headlong into Armstrong's raiders.

US Army Military History Institute

Aggressive patrolling by Colonel Manning Force of the Twentieth Ohio Infantry early on the morning of August 30 precipitated the battle of Middleburg.

3

'Give Them Cold Steel, Boys!'

The dawn of August 30 broke bright and clear. The cloudless sky gave evidence that there would be no relief from the heat and drought that plagued the area.

In Bolivar, just after dawn, a messenger from the provost marshal's office came to the home of John H. Bills, a local planter and businessman, and told him that four black men who claimed to be his slaves had been arrested as they tried to cross the Union lines into town. Bills was asked to come to the provost's office and identify these men. Dressing hurriedly, Bills walked down to the marshal's office and identified the men as his slaves, members of a work detail he had sent south to work his land in the vicinity of Hickory Valley near Middleburg.

The slaves were anxious to explain their presence in Bolivar and said that Confederate cavalry had run them off. The story sounded improbable to Bills, but the Union officers present began to question the men more closely. Under this questioning, the slaves said a great number of Southern cavalry had camped at LaGrange the day before and were headed north at that moment.[1]

This was not the first time the Federals had heard of Armstrong's presence, but it was certainly the best confirmed story. There had already been a report that a body of perhaps 400 Southern partisans had been seen north of Grand Junction and just south of the Union army's post at Middleburg.[2]

Bolivar's post commander, Colonel Marcellus Crocker, had been keeping a close watch on the situation to the south since Grant's dispatch five days before warning him of Armstrong's advance. But now that he had evidence confirming Confederate activity, he was not sure what to do.

Crocker, a native of Indiana, had only recently been given command at Bolivar. He had experience with railroad guard duty in Missouri early in the war and combat experience at Shiloh, where he commanded an Iowa regiment.[3] At his disposal were a large number of troops, but he did not know how many he should commit to a patrol south. The important facts to determine were how large a force he was facing and whether Bolivar was being threatened.

At seven o'clock that morning, Crocker called Colonel Mortimer Leggett of the Seventy-Eighth Ohio Infantry to his headquarters. Leggett, rough and well educated, had a reputation as a first-class officer and fighter. Born in New York state, he moved to Ohio at an early age and became a farmer and later a lawyer. At Bolivar, he commanded a "brigade" of unattached units made up primarily of his regiment and the Twentieth Ohio Infantry.[4]

Colonel Crocker told Leggett of his growing concern. By all accounts, there seemed to be a force of rebel cavalry just south of Bolivar, but their numbers and intent were unclear. Crocker proposed a reconnaissance in force. Leggett was ordered to take his two infantry regiments, along with two companies of the Eleventh Illinois Cavalry and a two-gun section of the Ninth Indiana Artillery, and push south of Middleburg, scouting out the country and engaging any partisan bands they might meet.[5]

If Bolivar was a nest of activity that morning, LaGrange presented the opposite picture. As dawn broke, Armstrong's men left camp and began to scout the surrounding countryside. Armstrong had found at roll call that morning that the lure of home was too strong for many of the more restive soldiers in his command. Several men, especially in the Tennessee regiments, were reported as being absent without leave. This was especially true of those units raised in West Tennessee who were going home for the first time in months. The Seventh Tennessee reported at least twenty-five men missing, including some officers. Even some of the Mississippi troopers had disappeared during the night.

Once an accurate roll call had been completed, Armstrong marched his men northeast toward Van Buren, a move that took him past the rail head at Grand Junction. Van Buren was a small farming community a few miles east of the Mississippi Central Railroad that led to Bolivar. Armstrong may have thought that he would be able to achieve an element of surprise by avoiding Union patrols along the railroad.

Back at Bolivar, Leggett was beginning to mobilize his forces. Union picket lines were located a mile out of town, where the Twentieth Ohio Infantry, under Colonel Manning Force, was waiting for the arrival of Leggett and his men.

Force was known as a capable officer and man of action. While on picket duty, the Twentieth Ohio had received reports of Confederate activity to their front. Anxious to know what was just beyond his lines, Force sent out two companies of his men under Major John Fry to "feel" for the enemy. This little force, mounted on mules, disappeared down the dusty road to Middleburg before Colonel Leggett arrived.[6]

Apprised of the situation, Leggett felt that Force's action was proper, and under the circumstances, he thought these men would make a good advance guard. He sent forty-five of his own men to reinforce Major Fry. These men were also on mules, a tactical concept in mounted infantry that Leggett had developed.[7]

Orders had been left for the cavalry and artillery to join Leggett at the Twentieth Ohio's picket post, but they were late in arriving. While they waited, Leggett and Force began to compare notes, and as they talked they became uneasier. They had heard too many reports of large groups of Confederate cavalry for these men to believe that the rebels were not intent on some major mischief. They became convinced that a large force of Southern cavalry was located somewhere just south of Middleburg.

Colonel Leggett now believed that the advance party had put itself in peril. He ordered Colonel Force to bring his regiment and three companies of the Seventy-Eighth Ohio forward as soon as the artillery arrived. Then leaving orders that the rest of the Seventy-Eighth Ohio should be ready to move at a moment's notice, he set off with his staff toward Middleburg to find Major Fry and prevent him from bringing on an engagement before the rest of the brigade could be brought up. It was too late.[8]

Armstrong's men had begun moving through Van Buren a little after daybreak. He had let the Seventh Tennessee Cavalry take the advance position because most of the men were familiar with the country. Riding through Van Buren, the rebels turned due north toward Middleburg. Armstrong hoped to burn the railroad station at Middleburg and run off any Union troops that were there. The town was the farthest point General Wheeler's July raid had reached, and Armstrong was intent on passing it.

Shortly before noon, the Tennesseans ran headlong into Major Fry's men on the old Van Buren road. Fry had turned toward Van Buren following local reports of Confederate activity. He was somewhat surprised when he came upon a dismounted skirmish line of Confederate cavalry just a few miles outside Middleburg.

A skirmish soon developed in the thick timber that lined each side of the Van Buren road. The action quickly turned into a determined but bloodless sniper's match.

When Leggett found Fry, he thought the force opposing them was only a little larger than his own advance guard. He immediately sent for reinforcements and was surprised when two companies of the Eleventh Illinois Cavalry arrived only a few minutes later. The cavalry, under the command of Major S. D. Puterbaugh, had left Bolivar ahead of the infantry and artillery by another road and happened to be on the scene of action when the call for reinforcements went out.

Puterbaugh tried to deploy his forty men, but the heavy timber prevented them from acting in a typical mounted cavalry role. Leggett ordered Puterbaugh to dismount his men and have them fight on foot as infantry since they could not be deployed on horseback, but, to his chagrin, he learned that only a dozen of these men had carbines. Only a few of the men in the Eleventh Illinois Cavalry had been issued longarms.[9]

Colonel Leggett cursed the fact that the heavy timber prevented him from deploying his cavalry and finding out the true strength of the Confederates. Yet, the heavy timber that prevented him from seeing the Southern forces was also preventing Armstrong from using his overwhelming forces to their best effect.

If Leggett was angered by the fact that he could not get a clear view of his enemy, then Armstrong was beside himself. If he could not get past this roadblock in the woods, his raid would be stillborn. Something had to give, and Armstrong believed he had found a solution. About a mile to the rear of the Confederate battle line was a large expanse of cotton fields and cleared ground. If Armstrong could lure the Federals into the open, he could jump them with his superior force. He communicated this plan to Colonel "Red" Jackson of the Seventh Tennessee and a withdrawal was ordered.

Suddenly, the Confederate skirmish line began to fall back, so Leggett ordered his men forward. The retreat continued at a walking pace as the rebels fell back to the support of their main force. For nearly a mile, the rebels fell back with Leggett closely following, until the woods thinned and, coming to the top of a ridge, he had a clear view of what lay before him. Stunned, he later reported, "I had a distinct view of the foe and found that I was contending with a force of over 6,000. . . ."[10]

Colonel Leggett realized he had found the force that Grant had warned of in his dispatch the week before. Staying within the woods so as to not expose his force to the Confederates, Leggett sent a desperate message to Colonel Crocker in Bolivar asking for all the reinforcements he could spare.

No one in Bolivar knew of the situation developing on the Van Buren road only a few miles to the south. At nine o'clock, the morning train arrived from Jackson bringing seven companies of the Second Illinois Cavalry. The Second Illinois had been sent to Bolivar under previous orders to patrol the railroad south of town. They had just returned from a successful series of actions that had cleared the railroad north of Jackson of partisan activity.[11]

The dashing Colonel Harvey Hogg, of Bloomington, Illinois, led the regiment. Hogg, a lawyer in civilian life, had earned a reputation of being a first-class cavalry officer, having distinguished himself at Fort Donelson and Shiloh, as well as for an action early in the war when he led his regiment in the capture of Columbus, Kentucky. Hogg was a traditionalist who always urged his men to use their sabers in close combat.[12]

When Colonel Crocker received Leggett's urgent request for reinforcements, he was in a tight spot. Crocker had suspected all along that Bolivar was the objective of this rebel advance. He also believed, falsely, that the force south of Bolivar was only the advance guard of a major Confederate army. As much as he wanted to help Leggett, he was afraid to abandon the fortifications at Bolivar. To Crocker, the recent arrival of Hogg's cavalry must have seemed a godsend.

Crocker ordered Hogg to reinforce Leggett's brigade, now concentrating on Middleburg. Hogg immediately left Bolivar with seven companies that in total numbered just over 130 men.[13]

Meanwhile, Armstrong was increasing the pressure on the Union force blocking the Van Buren road. Colonel Leggett faced what seemed like an impossible situation. Fearing the Confederates would learn his true strength and rush him, he was forced to keep his men in the woods. He knew he could not easily retreat from the fight without forfeiting his men, because the ground between his position and nearby Middleburg was open farmland, ideal for the enemy cavalry he now faced. He had one option, and that was to fight until help arrived.

His men had been fighting for more than an hour when Colonel Force arrived with six companies of the Twentieth Ohio and the two-gun section of the Ninth Indiana Artillery, under the command of Lieutenant W. Hight.[14]

Leggett threw forward the men of the Twentieth Ohio and took his own little advance guard out of action. These ninety men he would use as a mobile reserve and, if need be, rear guard.

The gun battery presented its own problems. The Ninth Indiana Artillery mounted twelve-pound howitzers. These smoothbore guns were the backbone of the army at that time. But like all field pieces of that era, they were aimed by line of sight, so the gunners had to see their target to aim and adjust their fire to make it accurate. In this battle, fought in tall timber, the gunners had no target unless they exposed themselves in the open. Besides, Leggett felt the battery had no proper infantry support to protect the guns once they were deployed. Rather than deploy the battery, he ordered it to the rear with instructions to remain limbered in case they had to beat a hasty retreat.

As Union resistance stiffened, Armstrong became annoyed. The dry weather had created a thick dust that was to plague both sides and play a part in the whole campaign. Scouts from Armstrong's force had noticed clouds of dust moving in the Union rear toward Middleburg for some time. The Federals were getting reinforcements, and if they were sufficient, Armstrong could be tied down in the woods and his great raid would come to naught.

Looking for a way to flank the Union force or get between them and their reinforcements, Armstrong ordered Colonel Robert McCulloch's regiment, the Second Missouri Cavalry, to move through the woods to the left, along with Colonel Slemons's Second Arkansas Cavalry, and find a way around the Union roadblock.[15]

McCulloch moved out, closely followed by Slemons, through the woods and across the Mississippi Central Railroad tracks to the Middleburg road, which ran between that town and Hickory Valley. Here, the Middleburg road ran in a southwesterly direction and, once gained, would put the Confederates in the rear of Colonel Leggett's men and between any help he might receive from Bolivar.

But once again, the thick dust clouds were betraying an army's movements. Alert Union soldiers had noticed a large dust cloud rising over the tree line and moving past their right flank. Leggett also saw this dust cloud and did not have to be told what it meant.

Immediately, Leggett ordered the artillery to the juncture of the Middleburg and Van Buren roads, where the guns were to be stationed to fire toward Middleburg. He then gave command of the forces on the Van Buren road over to Colonel Force with orders to hold at all costs. Then he personally took command of the mounted reserves and dashed away to Middleburg toward the advancing dust cloud.[16]

Racing southward down the main street of town, Leggett saw the Confederate cavalry emerging from the woods on the left side of the road. Seeking an advantageous spot for defense, he ordered his men to dismount and form a skirmish line behind a railroad embankment that ran parallel to the road on the right. From the security of this natural breastwork, the Federals opened up a galling fire on the Confederates.[17]

Charging from the woods by platoon, the advance guard of the Second Missouri fell on Leggett's little force. Leading the assault was Captain Rock Champion of Company K. Champion was a fire-eating secessionist and the hero of the regiment. The first man to engage the Federals, he was also the first to die, shot through the head at the beginning of the fight. Dispirited, the Confederates fell back to the safety of the woods and regrouped.[18]

Just at that moment, Captain Zachariah Chandler of the Seventy-Eighth Ohio arrived with companies E and C of that regiment and companies E and G of the Twentieth Ohio. Leggett ordered these men into line, having two companies form on the left side of the road and two on the right, thus hoping to keep the Confederates out of Middleburg. However, somehow in the heat of battle, Chandler got his orders confused and advanced down the road parallel to the Union position in the railroad cut. This exposed his right flank to the Southerners in the woods. At the embankment, Leggett's men shouted a warning and waved their hats, but Chandler's men mistook this for shouts of encouragement and began waving back. A sudden volley of fire from the woods woke them to the truth. Confederate fire ripped through the Union ranks, and Chandler was only able to rally the men once they fell back out of musket range.[19]

This brief exchange and the evident arrival of more Southern cavalry caused Leggett to abandon his position behind the embankment. His men now re-formed on Middleburg's main street, facing south. Chandler's men also redeployed. With two companies of the Twentieth Ohio on the left and two companies of the Seventy-Eighth Ohio on the right, he once again advanced down the road.

Firing as they advanced, the Union infantry soon passed the railroad embankment, driving a thin line of Southern skirmishers before them. On the right flank, the Union line came up against a stout fence and stopped. On the left, the Union line halted in a more exposed position at the edge of a large cotton field. Yet, for the time being, it was the right of Chandler's line that was bearing the brunt of the battle.[20]

Separated from the Union forces by a meadow and another stout fence, the Confederates exchanged heavy fire with Chandler's men on the right side of the road, so much so, in fact, that the Federals thought they might run out of ammunition.[21]

Then suddenly, along the woodline on the Confederate side, a large body of mounted men, at least a regiment in strength, appeared briefly from under the cover of the trees. Chandler's men were awestruck. The show of force was not lost on Leggett. Quickly, he sent requests for reinforcements both to Colonel Force on the Van Buren road and back to Bolivar. The rest of the Seventy-Eighth Ohio Infantry were on the road from Bolivar and reported that they were near at hand, yet it was evident these men would not arrive before the Confederates launched a major attack. Likewise, promises of support from Colonel Force were useless because he, too, was too far away.[22]

Soon a large force of Confederate cavalry emerged from the woods. Leggett had a feeling of impending doom, as it was obvious that the enemy was going to fall hard on his left flank, and there was nothing he could do to stop them. Behind the first body of Southern cavalry, another force could be seen advancing.

Colonel Bob McCulloch had surveyed the Union line from his position in the woods and had seen that on the left it did not extend far beyond the railroad embankment. Although the ground before the Union line was open, McCulloch knew that he had more than enough room to maneuver his regiment. He planned to hit the Union line on the left and roll it up away from Middleburg. In anticipation of a rout, he had ordered Slemons's Second Arkansas to follow him in supporting distance.

At that critical moment, help came from an unexpected quarter as the Second Illinois Cavalry arrived on the field. Colonel Hogg reported to Leggett. Because Colonel Force was still far from this portion of the battlefield, and the rest of the Seventy-Eighth Ohio was strung out on the road to Bolivar, Leggett had no choice but to send the Second Illinois to the extreme left to face the onslaught of two massed Confederate regiments.

Leggett ordered Hogg to the left but warned him, ". . . If you have any doubt about holding your position, you had better face back and not receive their charge."

Hogg seemed stung by the suggestion and retorted: "Colonel Leggett, for God's sake don't send me back."[23]

Hogg's resolve encouraged Leggett, so he ordered Hogg into position and told him, "Meet them with a charge, Colonel, and may heaven bless you."[24]

While this exchange was taking place, Missouri troopers could be seen kicking down the fence that separated the wide cotton field in front of the Union battle line from their position at the edge of the woods. Their regiment, then deployed in a long line of battle, thundered through the gaps in the fence and "faced right" toward the railroad embankment. With McCulloch at their head, the Missourians drew their sabers and charged forward. Slemons's Arkansas troops followed close behind, formed a line just in front of the destroyed fence, and halted.

Just then, Hogg's men filed past the railroad embankment and formed a line just south of it. Seeing the Confederates rush forward, Hogg drew his sword and urged his men forward with the cry, "Give them cold steel, boys!"[25]

Colonel Hogg rode boldly ahead of his men, conspicuous in a white shirt, with his officer's jacket tied across the pommel of his saddle. He immediately sought out Colonel McCulloch, who himself was a conspicuous figure as he was attired in a full dress uniform. The two men engaged in hand-to-hand combat.[26]

The opposing regiments crashed together in a fight Leggett later described as "sublimely terrible."[27] The thunder of the horses' hooves, the slashing of the sabers, scattered pistol shots, and the cries of the wounded rent the summer air. Those soldiers not directly engaged looked on, spellbound, at the spectacle before them.

Hogg, the younger man, bore down on McCulloch and seemed to be getting the upper hand when a Missouri trooper rode to his colonel's aid. Riding alongside Colonel Hogg, the gray-clad rider pressed a pistol into the Union colonel's side and pulled the trigger. The gun fired with a loud report and Hogg's white shirt blotched red. At the same moment, another shot struck Hogg's horse square in the forehead, and both man and horse collapsed in a heap on the ground. With sheer determination, Hogg stood up, his saber dangling from his right hand and his dead horse's reins in his left. Another shot rang out and Hogg fell dead, with a bullet through his brain.[28]

The Union cavalry, now leaderless, cut their way through the Second Missouri's line, only to find themselves faced by Slemons's Second Arkansas. Out of this confusion, Captain M. H. Musser of Company F brought some order to the Illinois troopers and ordered them to cut their way back to the Union lines.

The irascible Colonel Slemons was beside himself with anger. He had seen the Union cavalrymen cut their way through the vaunted Missouri cavalry and now they were turning their backs to his men, a maneuver he thought was done in pure contempt.

Waving his sword over his head, Slemons spurred his horse and galloped toward the enemy. Suddenly conscious of the fact he had given his men no orders, he shouted over his shoulder, "Charge them, damn their American hearts, charge them!"[29]

The Arkansas troopers surged forward and slammed into the rear of the Second Illinois, and the Second Illinois in turn plowed back through the Second Missouri's disorganized line.

Now a wild melee broke out. Several companies of the Second Arkansas, trying to follow the original battle plan, rode past the mingled cavalry and attacked the Union infantry around the railroad embankment, but all was lost for the moment. The remaining men from Chandler's Union infantry raced back to Middleburg but were not followed. The Missourians were hopelessly mixed up with the Arkansas troops, and the sheer audacity of Hogg's charge had left them bewildered. McCulloch ordered the bugles to sound retreat, and the Confederates fell back to the safety of the woods. Slemons, however, still full of fight, thought the retreat was too hasty and later wrote, "They (McCulloch's regiment) gave way and left men in the field alone."[30]

A strange quiet now fell over the battlefield. A number of prisoners had been taken and Slemons was proud that his men and their "long-haired, ugly Arkansas colonel"[31] had gained new respect. He learned from one of the captured Federal cavalrymen that his men had engaged the Second Illinois Cavalry. He immediately inquired of their Colonel Hogg. Slemons wrote years later that Hogg's death was one of the most regrettable facts of the war. Slemons and Hogg had been friends before the war, graduating from the same law class at Cumberland University.[32]

When Confederate troopers noticed that hogs were rooting around the fallen colonel, they placed his body over a fence to keep it off the ground. Later, under a flag of truce, Colonel Hogg's body was carried to the Union lines. A special pass had been granted to a Missouri trooper to accompany the body back to Illinois; that Confederate trooper was Harvey Hogg's only brother.[33]

The lull had lasted for the better part of an hour. As the field was being cleared of the dead and wounded, Colonel Force arrived with his men. With some forethought, Force had brought the artillery with him. Then, as if by design, seven companies of the Seventy-Eighth Ohio, under the command of Major D. F. Carnahan, arrived on the battlefield. Now, for the first time that day, Leggett had his entire brigade in one place.[34]

He ordered his men to form a new line of battle just northwest of

Middleburg. Leggett was now somewhat secure in his new position.

Leaving his forces on the Van Buren road under the command of Colonel Jackson, General Armstrong rode to the scene of action to take personal command. He also brought the Third Tennessee Cavalry to reinforce McCulloch's men.[35] By now, McCulloch and Slemons had rallied and separated their jumbled units. Confidently, they came out of the woods and formed a broad line of battle in the contested cotton field in preparation for an attack on the now "retreating" Federals.

Instead, the Ninth Indiana Artillery opened up on them. Although the shells did little damage, their presence on the battlefield kept the Confederates at bay and finally caused them to fall back to the safety of the woods.

Convinced that the Confederates would not follow him too closely, Leggett ordered a retreat to Bolivar. The battle of Middleburg was over. A veteran of the Twentieth Ohio said the fight had severely tested the regiment and it was with great effort that the regiment ". . . all fagged out, dragged itself back into town."[36]

Colonel Leggett felt lucky to have gotten his men out of Middleburg and back to Bolivar. They had fought well in that daylong, confusing battle, and he could not have expected more. His report, written and submitted to Colonel Crocker at Bolivar, praised the efforts of his men and especially the merits of several junior officers.

General Armstrong's appraisal of what happened that day was dictated by the display of courage he saw around him. He had not brought his entire force to bear on the Union brigade at Middleburg, nor did he seem to want to do so. The Second Tennessee, Wirt Adams's Battalion, and the First Mississippi regiment had not been engaged that day, although they had spent the day mounted and within hearing of the developing battle. The failure of Armstrong to fully deploy his forces may have been due to the rugged terrain; it was certainly not a ploy. If he had hoped to deceive the Federals as to his strength, he had already been found out, since Leggett had seen his entire force on the Van Buren road.

Inspired by Grant's warnings, Leggett had overestimated

Armstrong's numbers, which in turn caused Colonel Crocker to draw the Union forces back into Bolivar to await the assault of a rebel army that did not exist. The Union army was playing into Armstrong's hand.

Once the details of the battle were known, Southern papers were quick to praise Armstrong.

> "Throughout the action, General Armstrong showed himself to be the finest cavalry officer in our service. He handles cavalry on the field as well as Beauregard handles infantry. His men are devoted to him beyond anything I ever heard of. On the field he is cool and collected and moves his men as Morphy moves his chessmen. Take my word for it, Frank Armstrong, brigadier general of cavalry, is one of the greatest captains of the war, and with opportunity, will palce [sic] himself with Stonewall Jackson, or in front of him."[37]

Despite such glowing reports by enthusiastic reporters, this new Stonewall Jackson was at a crossroads. It was true he had defeated a large force of the enemy, but this was not what his mission was about. He had come to raid the enemy's supply lines, and this was a task he had not yet begun.

US Army Military History Institute

Colonel Mortimer Leggett of the Seventy-Eighth Ohio Infantry was ordered to sweep the area south of Bolivar on August 30. His force would become heavily engaged before nightfall.

US Army Military History Institute

Instead of being granted a leave to go home due to illness, Union General Leonard Fulton Ross found himself commanding the District of West Tennessee at the time of Armstrong's Raid.

4

The Race to Medon Station

Military dispatches had arrived for General Leonard Fulton Ross earlier that day while the battle at Middleburg was still raging and the civilian population of the town was "in a great state of excitement."[1]

Ross was somewhat perplexed by the situation. He was not well and only the month before had asked for a leave of absence from his post at Bolivar because of an undiagnosed fever. Instead, his superiors sent him to Jackson to recuperate and then named him commander of the area.[2]

As it stood, Ross was, for better or worse, the commander of the whole District of West Tennessee. Both of his immediate superiors, General John McClernand and General John Logan, were away in Illinois recruiting or furthering their political careers, leaving Ross as the district's senior officer.

After a conference that afternoon, Crocker and Ross concurred that Bolivar was under immediate threat of attack. The defenses of Bolivar had been under construction for some months. Slave labor, or rather contraband labor, had been used to construct a series of earthworks, stockades, and forts north of town. Ross felt the place could be held, and Colonel Crocker, now in the post that Ross had once held, swore that it would be held.

As afternoon wore into night, the tired veterans of Leggett's brigade came straggling into town. His men were whipped, if not militarily, at least physically. The heat and exertions of the day had taken a terrible toll.

The Second Illinois Cavalry had taken the worst beating of the battle that afternoon, and they were shattered. They counted six dead, including their colonel; two dozen wounded; and a large number taken prisoner. The artillery arrived intact, and the infantry, although bloodied, was still full of fight. Ross had counted on these men being in shape to withstand the Confederate attack expected in the morning.

Throughout the night, they waited. The Southern cavalry had followed Leggett closely as he retreated toward Bolivar, but never to the point of bringing on another engagement.[3] Tension in the Union ranks was palpable as the garrison was ordered to sleep on its arms that night.

Dawn of August 31 broke clear and quiet. A little after sunrise, General Ross decided it would be better if the garrison showed a little fight, so an hour after daybreak, the whole division of 7,000 men was called out and marched a mile south of town to form a battle line across the Middleburg road. One hour passed, then two, without the sight of a single Confederate.[4]

Curious, Ross ordered a cavalry patrol south. They found nothing. From Bolivar to Middleburg and from Middleburg south, there was not a single Confederate to be found. The 6,000 men Leggett had reported fighting the day before had vanished into thin air.

Colonel Crocker began to think that this was some sort of Confederate trick. General Ross began to suspect the worst. If Bolivar was not threatened, then what was? He suddenly realized that if Bolivar had been bypassed, then the Southern forces were striking further north. Jackson, the headquarters of the district, with its huge supply depots and under-strength garrison, was the target.

Ross rode quickly to the train depot in Bolivar and commandeered the morning train going north to Jackson. He ordered the men of Company H of the Eleventh Iowa Infantry, who were guarding the train station, to board the train with him and act as his guard. Ross knew he must get to Jackson at the earliest possible moment to organize a defense. The race was on.[5]

Having followed the Union retreat into Bolivar, General Armstrong had two options open to him. He could proceed with an attack on the town or he could bypass that garrison and go on to his ultimate goal of Jackson.

There was a good argument for bypassing Bolivar, as it was heavily fortified and strongly garrisoned. Armstrong had felt from the first that the town was not an important objective in his campaign; rather, he saw it as a roadblock to be passed. In a dispatch to General Price, Armstrong stated that he had decided not to attack Bolivar because the garrison, dug in and desperate, might shell the town and cause civilian casualties.[6] But his magnanimous act may have been done more to spare his own men than out of a concern for the civilian populace.

Believing their intelligence reports of an advancing Southern army, the garrison at Bolivar was frozen in place. Armstrong was able to move unmolested around the town and head north. The Confederates began their flanking movement around Bolivar at sundown the day of the Middleburg fight. By nine o'clock, Armstrong's whole command was camped on the banks of Clearwater Creek, west of Bolivar and just south of the Hatchie River.[7]

Based on reports from his scouts, Armstrong knew a Federal unit stationed at Estanaula controlled all the fords and crossings of the Hatchie River in this area. According to the reports, this garrison consisted of a regiment of infantry supported by a two-gun section of artillery. These fords were vital to Armstrong's plans because they provided access to the northern half of West Tennessee and a route south once the raid was over.

By two o'clock in the morning, Armstrong once again had his men on the march. As he sought a way across the Hatchie, he found that he was aided by the weather. The river was so low that he could cross it just about anywhere, so the Confederates would not have to force a crossing. Armstrong chose to cross the Hatchie at the mouth of Clover Creek, the very spot where, only two weeks before, Colonel Dennis had speculated a large force could cross. By doing so, Armstrong had placed himself between Dennis's men at Estanaula and any hope of reinforcement that the garrison might draw from Bolivar or Jackson.[8]

A short time after Armstrong's men had crossed the Hatchie, a civilian rode up to Dennis's headquarters outside Estanaula and told him that the Confederates had crossed the Hatchie and he and his garrison were in grave danger.[9]

Dennis reacted quickly and decisively. He roused his men and ordered them to make ready for a forced night march to Jackson, his only avenue of escape. He then commandeered all the wagons in the area, forty in number, and loaded them with all the vital supplies he could carry. What could not be carried was piled up and burned to keep it from the hands of the enemy. This proved to be no easy task since the garrison had been resupplied only the day before.

The regimental historian of the Thirtieth Illinois recalled one particular incident that night with relish: "This was on a Sunday morning, and about Friday before our teams had been to Jackson for provisions, and two barrels of whiskey was in the supply. We hurriedly packed our knapsacks and loaded the wagons with camp equipage. The two barrels of whiskey was cumbersome for troops on a forced march. The heads were knocked in and the barrels upset and the whiskey went on the ground. The boys could not stand to see a waste such as that, and they got busy dipping it up in their hands and drinking it, and went on their way rejoicing."[10]

No sooner had Dennis started for Jackson than he met a dispatch rider from General Ross's headquarters ordering him to carry out the very measures he had just undertaken. Ross also instructed that Dennis should march straight to Jackson and reinforce the garrison there.[11] Dennis's men started their long march looking over their shoulders lest the Confederate cavalry catch them from the rear.

Meanwhile, on the north side of the Hatchie, Armstrong divided his forces. He sent two regiments, the First Mississippi and Wirt

Adams's Cavalry Battalion, under the overall command of Colonel Pinson, straight toward Estanaula in an effort to cut off the garrison there and capture the crossing. As the Mississippi troops set off, Armstrong rode with the rest of his command toward Toone station, several miles to the east. His forces, spearheaded by the Second Tennessee Cavalry, avoided the main roads and made their way northeast through the fields and woods.[12]

Toone was occupied by five companies of the Forty-Fifth Illinois Infantry under the leadership of Colonel Jasper Maltby. Earlier that morning, a train arrived in Toone station carrying General Ross to Jackson. Ross told Maltby of the situation at Bolivar and warned him that the Confederates were probably on their way there and to keep a sharp eye out for them.[13]

Maltby asked Ross to carry the word farther up the line to the regiment's detachments at Treadger and Medon Station. To facilitate this, Maltby ordered the Forty-Fifth's regimental adjutant, Captain William Frolock, to board the train and accompany the general.

Their rush north, however, was almost immediately delayed by sabotage, much to the embarrassment of Colonel Maltby. The station's water tower hose had been stuffed with rags, and the exasperated Federals had to take the better part of an hour to clear it. The delay cost Ross some precious time. As the tower was within sight of Maltby's headquarters, security obviously had been lax.

Maltby immediately ordered his men to prepare a defense of the town. Since they had been stationed in a rear area, the 210 men had never made provisions for defense. There were no blockhouses or breastworks at Toone, but there was an abundance of cotton bales at the freight depot, so a barricade of cotton bales was erected around the passenger depot.[14]

Ross's train, now watered and fueled, had not pulled out of sight of the station when the Toone garrison lost telegraph communication with Bolivar to the south. This meant, in all likelihood, that the Confederates were across the Hatchie.

Back at Estanaula, Pinson's forces learned from the local civilians that the Union garrison had retreated toward Jackson early that morning. Since they could not salvage any of the supplies destroyed by Dennis, and since the Estanaula ford was now cleared of Federal troops, Pinson decided to turn his men north and rejoin Armstrong and the main body of troops.

Just before noon, the Second Tennessee attacked and drove in the pickets at Toone. Armstrong, sizing up the situation, did not attack the barricaded garrison but made a show of force by marching around the town in plain view of the defenders. Maltby then learned that he had lost contact with his men at Treadger, a few miles to the north.[15] This display of force by the Confederates convinced Maltby that the Southern cavalry was the advance guard of Price's entire army. His men expected momentarily to see infantry and artillery surround the town. Luther Cowan, an officer of the Forty-Fifth Illinois stationed at Toone, wrote to his wife about that morning: "It is the time for the greatest anxiety for us. We are well fortified with cotton bales, two hundred and ten fighting men. We can hold the place against any number of infantry that can be sent against us, but if they get us with artillery, they will surely clean us out."[16]

For reasons known only to Armstrong, he did not ask for the surrender of the Federal garrison at Toone. After his men rode around the town in parade formation, they disappeared into the woods northwest of town, leaving Maltby to wonder if this was some sort of "rebel trick."

At Treadger station, just a few miles north, where Company C of the Forty-Fifth Illinois was camped, Ross's train sped past. Adjutant Frolock tossed a piece of kindling off the engine to the nearest soldier to the track. A note attached to the wood apprised the men there of the situation and asked them to be extra alert. What they did not know was that, at that moment, less than a mile away, the advance guard of the Confederates were riding "hell for leather" to capture Ross's train.

The train bearing Ross had just disappeared from sight when, with a wild whoop, the Confederate cavalry came crashing out of the nearby woods. Shouting and shooting, they charged down the track straight at the railroad guard.

Company C quickly formed behind a makeshift barricade of railroad crossties and delivered a ragged volley of fire at the gray-clad horsemen, but the rebels rode around this obstacle and surrounded the garrison. Company C was captured in total.[17]

The brief struggle at Treadger cost the Confederates four wounded and the Federals one killed, two wounded, and forty captured. Armstrong set fire to the long trestle, the nearby wood yard, and two cars of cotton sitting on a sidetrack, then rode north.

At Toone, Colonel Maltby was anxious for his men strung out along the track, and he was especially worried about those at Treadger. Calling for volunteers, Maltby ordered Company B, reinforced by those who would go, to bring back Company C and scout for the enemy. By the time this relief force arrived at Treadger, it was too late; the place was on fire, and the only sign of Company C was the body of a dead private lying beside the track.[18]

The would-be rescuers turned and quietly crept back into their fortified position at Toone. By then, Ross's train had made it to the next station, Medon, and stopped. Ross warned the men there that the Confederates were probably somewhere just south of town and might attack the station. Captain Frolock got off the train and helped organize a defense. Medon Station was garrisoned by four companies of the Forty-Fifth Illinois Infantry under the command of Captain James Palmer, in all approximately 120 men. Just as at the other depots, a great deal of cotton lay about the freight station. The men were ordered to use the cotton bales to build a barricade around the passenger station and the telegraph office, their main point of defense. General Ross stayed long enough to see the work begun and then continued north by train to Jackson.[19]

The Iowa soldiers aboard Ross's train had hoped their ride to Jackson would be uneventful, but their sense of urgency grew with each successive stop along the way. The faint, distant sound of gunfire behind them only underlined this feeling.

Once they reached Jackson, Ross immediately went to his headquarters, and the unhappy Iowa boys were ordered to stay aboard and protect the train on its return trip to Bolivar.

Just before noon, the train went back through Medon headed toward Bolivar, but at the first stop, they found the garrison tense. Since Ross's train had passed through that morning, there had been reports that the Confederates were just south of Medon setting fire to trestles. Still, it was believed that this was only a force of partisan rangers emboldened by Armstrong's actions south of the Hatchie.[20]

Company A of the Forty-Fifth Illinois, under command of Captain Palmer, climbed aboard the train to ride as far as Treadger station with the Iowa troops. They had lost telegraph communication with that point just a bit earlier.

The train had gone about two miles south of Medon when it came upon a burning trestle. Immediately, the soldiers jumped off the train and put out the fire. No sooner had this been done than their attention was drawn to a bridge about half a mile farther down the track. Southern cavalry could be seen defiantly setting fire to this structure in clear view of the train's guard.

Angered by the Confederates' seeming contempt, the men of the Iowa company pushed forward, closely followed by the Illinois soldiers. Veterans of Shiloh, the Iowa troops were desperately trying to close with the elusive enemy. Occasionally, they would flush a rebel picket from his post along the track and chase him off with a volley of shots.

If it all seemed too easy for the Federals, it was meant to be. Neither Captain Palmer nor his Iowa counterpart, Captain Ben Beach, suspected an ambush, but that is just what happened. One of the Iowa soldiers described it this way: "Suddenly, and as unexpected as a flash of lighting [sic] in a blue sky, the brush on our right, about sixty yards ahead, glowed with a sheet of fire, and whiz-z-z, whiz-z-z came a perfect storm of bullets, singing about their heads, striking the railroad track, and tearing up the dust all around us! . . . We were ambushed."[21]

One man was killed and five wounded in the single volley of fire. The blue coats returned fire as best they could and retreated toward the train. But aboard the train, the crew had other ideas. Backing the train up the track toward Medon, they fled from the retreating soldiers and did not stop until they reached Jackson. The Federals, thus abandoned, took to the woods near the track and fought their way back to Medon in a hot, running gun battle.

Once again, the weather played a part in the action. A number of the retreating Federals fell out from heat exhaustion in the retreat. The group was determined to leave no one behind for the enemy to capture, and each affected man was bathed in water from their comrades' canteens and encouraged to continue. Likewise, the wounded were carried along in an effort to keep the group together.[22]

For what seemed like an eternity, the group kept up its retreat, fighting a stiff rearguard action. They managed to avoid any further casualties and were relieved when they finally drew within sight of Medon Station. At Medon, they quickly joined the force at the passenger station, a rather crude affair of oak clapboard that measured twenty by sixty feet.

The garrison prepared for a siege. Water was brought into the station and a railcar full of provisions was brought alongside the station platform.

The ambush south of Medon was a well-planned tactic, but the trap had been sprung too early. The plan had called for the ambush and capture of the train, but someone had been trigger-happy. One Confederate involved in the incident summed up the fight this way in a letter to his wife: "Heard a train coming ambushed it and if the goose in command had only torn up the track behind would have burned it . . ."[23]

Undaunted by the failure of their trap, the Confederates now converged on Medon Station.

At Medon, Adjutant Frolock took command from Captain Palmer, who had been wounded in the ambush, and ordered Sergeant David Williams and five men to the small trestle over Clover Creek, just south of town, as a lookout. As soon as this little party moved into position, they saw a large number of gray-clad horsemen advancing toward them up track. Williams knew that it was too far to run back to town and the Confederates were too strong to meet in the open. Spotting an abandoned cabin near the tracks, he ordered his men inside. Once there, they barricaded the door and opened fire on the advancing Southerners.

Once again, the men of the Second Tennessee, spearheading Armstrong's advance, found themselves under fire. Company A, sharpshooters armed with Enfield rifles, dismounted and returned fire. Meanwhile, the rest of the regiment tried to avoid the skirmish by riding farther to the east, but they soon found themselves under fire from Union soldiers hiding behind buildings in nearby Medon.[24]

When Frolock heard Williams's men shooting, he sent several more men to the south end of town to snipe at the rebels, hoping to buy time for the station's defenders, who were still working on the makeshift breastwork of cotton bales around the depot.

Command of the Second Tennessee had fallen to Major George Morton, an English citizen, after Colonel Barteau became ill and was forced to return to Mississippi. Sensing that the sniping was a delaying tactic, Morton took the greater part of the regiment and struck out to the northeast, avoiding the town. Once out of rifle range, Morton marched his command around the town, trying to gain the enemy rear by coming into it from the north.

The station lay ahead and Morton ordered a charge just as the Federals were heaving the last bales of their barricade into place. They had seen the Confederates bearing down on them just in time. The combat was brief and bloody, as the rebel charge broke against the barricade. Quickly realizing that he was accomplishing nothing, Morton ordered a withdrawal back out of rifle range, where his men dismounted.

Now on foot, the Confederates worked their way into Medon and captured some of the Union snipers in outlying buildings, in house-to-house fighting. Soon the Federals in the depot were surrounded. Back at the cabin south of town, Sergeant Williams and his men surrendered, having run out of ammunition.

By now, Armstrong had arrived with the greater part of his command. He sized up the situation from Morton's report of the fighting and ordered Colonel "Red" Jackson's Seventh Tennessee to dislodge the Federals from their fort. The first four companies of the regiment dismounted and formed for a charge south of the depot, masked by a large, brick Methodist church. From this position, they made a determined assault but ran into a hail of bullets from the station's more desperate defenders. Company C of the Seventh lost 25 percent of its men, killed and wounded within five minutes. The other companies fared little better. Their charge broken up, the Confederates retreated to the safety of nearby buildings, from which they kept up a steady fire on the Union garrison.[25]

Meanwhile, at Jackson, Ross tried to organize a defense of the city. Allen Geer, a soldier detailed to an army hospital in Jackson, recorded in his diary the effect General Ross's arrival had on the town: "Jackson was deemed in danger of attack and the greatest activity prevailed in putting the city in a state of defense. The stored cotton here is being constricted into forts and into barricades in the streets. Capt. Pullen assisted in arming the convalescents . . ."[26]

As defense preparations continued in Jackson, Ross began to consider a new plan. He was concerned about the town's ability to hold off a Confederate assault, even to the point of arming the ambulatory patients in the Army hospitals. Ross thought that if he could get the Confederates to spend their strength outside of Jackson, then the town would not be attacked. He reasoned that if he could keep the rebels occupied at Medon, then he might be able to deliver a blow to their rear. Caught between the garrison at Medon and an attacking force from Jackson, Armstrong could be crushed.

The only force left to Ross to deliver that blow to the Confederate rear at Medon was Dennis's little brigade on the road between Jackson and Estanaula. In the meantime, Ross needed to make sure Medon held out. To this end, he decided to send a newly formed regiment, the Seventh Missouri Infantry, to Medon with orders to engage the enemy and keep contact with him, while at the same time reinforcing the garrison there.

The Seventh Missouri, under the command of Major W. S. Oliver, was among the few complete combat units at Jackson at the time. This untried regiment was an independent command that had been sent to Jackson to await orders for combat duty with Grant at

Vicksburg. Seven hundred and thirty men strong, they would form the linchpin of Ross's battle plans.[27]

By early afternoon, the Seventh Missouri had boarded a special train headed toward Medon.

At the same time, Armstrong, with the town of Medon surrounded, was at a loss as to what to do. He apparently lost interest in capturing the town. Fighting had stopped and the two sides were content to stand and watch each other from their respective vantage points.

The train bearing the Seventh Missouri had traveled to within a mile of Medon when a cautious Major Oliver ordered it to stop. Leaving the train, the Missourians formed a line of battle, fixed bayonets, and began a slow advance down the tracks toward the town. Somehow, the Confederates remained unaware of the Union regiment's approach. Suddenly, with a shout, the Missourians came charging into town from the north, quickly fighting their way to the depot. The rebels offered little resistance. A few Confederates were captured, and only one Missourian was wounded.[28]

Having relieved the besieged garrison, the Seventh Missouri found themselves in a peculiar position because even though they had won back Medon, like their comrades in the Forty-Fifth Illinois, they were virtual prisoners inside the town. Surrounded by Armstrong's greatly superior force, they had been swallowed up, but in a larger sense, they were fulfilling Ross's orders of maintaining contact.

Colonel Dennis and his brigade were within five miles of Jackson when he received new orders from General Ross. He was to countermarch his command through Denmark, and from Denmark march to Medon. At Medon, he was to attack the rebel forces besieging the town. If, on the other hand, the Confederates had already taken the town, he was to immediately fall back to Jackson.[29] It is not recorded what Dennis thought of these new orders; after all, he had until this moment been fleeing Armstrong's superior numbers. Yet, Dennis did as he was ordered, and nightfall found him and his exhausted men camped at Denmark.

At Toone, Colonel Maltby was desperate to learn all he could about the fighting that was going on all around him. The telegraph wires had been cut, so he sent couriers north seeking news. He knew from other riders coming south that his men at Medon were under attack.

The dangerous job of dispatch rider was given to volunteers. Jimmy Harding, a private in Company B, Forty-Fifth Illinois, had been killed that morning trying to get a message through to Medon. A courier from Jackson who got through to Toone said all the roads were filled with rebel patrols and ambushes.[30]

Maltby, more anxious than ever, stoically remained in Toone. He still thought the place was in danger of attack from a Confederate army. All he could do was stay and wait to be relieved.

As night approached, General Armstrong was reinforced by the Mississippi regiments under Colonel Pinson. The Medon garrison saw the arrival of Pinson's men and believed this was in preparation for an all-out attack on their positions. But no attack developed and the garrison stood down as the rebels could clearly be seen pulling back into the countryside west of town.

During the night, Armstrong decided to continue the raid. During the previous two days, he had cut rail and telegraph communications between Jackson and Bolivar, he had defeated the enemy in battle at Middleburg, and he was now just ten miles from the supply depots at Jackson. The next day, his command would march westward toward the town of Denmark, then strike north to Jackson. After burning the depots there, he would backtrack through Denmark, move to Estanaula, and from there march back to Mississippi.

As dawn broke September 1, the Confederates began to move out. The Second Missouri took the advance guard position, followed by the First Mississippi and then the main body of Confederate troops. They chose the direct route to Denmark, marching down the old Medon road to the Steam Mill Ferry road. From there, they would turn down a little-known farm path called Britton's Lane to Denmark.

Major Oliver of the Seventh Missouri watched as the rebels rode out of sight and realized Ross's plans were going awry. He knew he must tie up Armstrong's men, but how? Finally, he came up with a simple idea; he would offer battle.

With drums beating, the Seventh Missouri marched out of

Medon and formed a line of battle in an open field west of town. The Confederates took no notice. Oliver was persistent, and his men advanced. In his zeal to execute Ross's order to maintain contact, Oliver had made a grave mistake. Without cavalry or artillery to support him, he marched beyond the point that the Medon garrison could come to his aid if he was attacked. He maneuvered his regiment through the fields as if on dress parade, oblivious to the jeopardy in which he had put his men.

Several of the Confederates watching were surprised at the Union major's lack of caution, but what was more surprising to them was that Armstrong did not attack. Instead, he ordered a few men to remain behind to watch the Union forces and continued his march to Jackson.[31]

The Federals continued their advance until they were far outdistanced by the Confederate cavalry. Unable to keep up, an exasperated Major Oliver halted his men and countermarched back to Medon.

At Denmark, Colonel Dennis roused his men and began his march toward Medon. A local pro-Union civilian who was familiar with the countryside had proposed to act as a guide for the Federals. Dennis confided his orders to the guide and his planned route of march. Noting the condition of Dennis's men after two days of hard marching, the civilian told Dennis of a shortcut to Medon that would take three miles from their planned route. The shortcut was down a farm road called Britton's Lane. Dennis assented to this change of route, knowing the importance of reaching Medon while the Confederates were still there.[32]

Now, as the morning turned into midday, the Union and Confederate forces began marching toward each other, each unaware of the other's presence. The stage was set for battle.

US Military History Institute

At Medon, Adjutant William Frolock (above) took command from Captain Palmer, who had been wounded in the ambush, and ordered Sergeant David Williams and five men to the small trestle over Clover Creek, just south of town, as a lookout.

US Army Military History Institute

Colonel Wirt Adams led the battalion that bore his name in a charge that captured the Union artillery at Britton's Lane. Casualties were staggering.

5

'Oh, Such Carnage'

Colonel Dennis set out from Denmark in the following order of march: in the advance guard was Company H, Twelfth Illinois Cavalry, followed by the Twentieth Illinois Infantry, Battery E, Second Illinois Artillery, the baggage train, and the Thirtieth Illinois Infantry. Captain Foster's Fourth Ohio Cavalry brought up the rear. Foster, who had some experience as a staff officer, accompanied Dennis, who rode in front of the Twentieth Illinois.[1]

Dennis had received reports during the night that the Confederates had been seen in great numbers at Estanaula. He feared the rebels had passed him during the night, so he ordered the Fourth Ohio Cavalry to scout toward Estanaula to check out these reports. Meanwhile, he continued his march toward Medon.[2]

The Union troops spread out along the road as they marched. The heat and the rigors of marching for the past two days were taking their toll. The Thirtieth Illinois began to fall far behind, a fact that concerned Dennis, who called for a brief rest to give the stragglers time to catch up.

Ordered to scout ahead, the troopers of the Twelfth Illinois, under the command of Lieutenant Charles O'Connell, followed the civilian guide's directions and turned into Britton's Lane.

The lane ran in an east-west direction through a section of broken country, intersected a ridge, and then dropped from the ridge into a small, fertile valley below. Along the ridge, they passed a few cabins, including one used as a school. East of this spot, the land was cultivated. The fields on the north side of the road were in corn. Half a mile east of the ridge, the lane intersected Steam Mill Ferry Road and the farm of Thomas Britton, after whom the lane was named. Two hundred yards away, the Medon road intersected Steam Mill Ferry Road, making a four-road junction.

Since crossing the ridge that morning, the Twelfth Illinois had noticed a cloud of dust in the east moving in their direction. By the time the Federals reached the crossroads, it was apparent that the dust cloud was the main body of Armstrong's force. Sizing up the situation, O'Connell sent one man back to tell Dennis to bring up his men as quickly as possible.[3] Meanwhile, fearing he could not outrun the Confederates, O'Connell decided to make a fight of it.

A small, wooded area, nearly circular in shape, stood at the southwest junction of the Medon and Steam Mill Ferry roads. O'Connell ordered his men to dismount and take cover in the timber. His forty men did not have long to wait for the Confederates. As the gray-clad riders approached from the east, the Federal cavalrymen formed a thin skirmish line among the trees.

The Second Missouri Cavalry under Colonel "Black Bob" McCulloch had led Armstrong's advance. The Missourians approached the crossroads slowly and cautiously. They, too, had seen a cloud of dust in the distance, this one raised by the Twelfth Illinois. While still at some distance from the woods, some of McCulloch's men were ordered to dismount and form a skirmish line across the Medon road.

Charles Prindle, a private in the Illinois cavalry, was known as a crack marksman back home in South Elgin, Illinois. Raising his carbine to his shoulder, he remarked to those around him that he had never shot a man before, but now he was going to try. His target was a mounted officer behind the advancing Confederate skirmish line. Although his target was nearly out of range, he fired and the man toppled from his horse. This was the first shot fired at the battle of Britton's Lane. Lieutenant O'Connell looked at his watch, and it was exactly 10 a.m.[4]

Prindle's shot was answered by dozens of Confederate rifles. At first, Armstrong, who had just arrived on the scene, thought the skirmishing was light and felt that the Union force must be small to stay within the confines of the woods.

Coming up behind the Missouri troopers was the First Mississippi Cavalry. The Mississippians did not become involved in the skirmish between their comrades and the Federals but were ordered by Armstrong to remain mounted, support the Missourians, and capture the Northerners once they were flushed from the woods.

Now the Seventh Tennessee Cavalry arrived and found the road blocked by the Mississippi troopers. They could hear the fight going on in their front but could not see what was happening. Colonel Jackson, of the Seventh Tennessee, ordered his men to dismount and walk their horses into a pasture off the north side of the Medon road. The men enjoyed their respite from riding in the heavy dust. They talked and smoked while waiting for the roadblock ahead to be cleared.[5]

Meanwhile, behind the Union-held woods, reinforcements were on the way. Captain Foster was leading the Twentieth Illinois to the scene of battle with Lieutenant Dengel and his artillery close behind. Colonel Dennis had reached the ridgeline ahead of them all, however, and was devising a battle plan.[6]

Instead of ordering his men to go to the woods at the east end of the lane in full view of the Confederates, he had them form a battle line in the timber at the foot of the ridge. Dennis knew he was greatly outnumbered and that his men were badly scattered. He understood that, once committed to battle, he could not easily disengage and make a run for Jackson, because most of his men were infantry and the rebel cavalry could easily run them down. His only choice, therefore, was to stay put and choose the most advantageous ground, in the hope that he could hold out until reinforcements arrived or fight his way out.

As the Twentieth Illinois came up, Dennis and Captain Foster led them into line. The whole ridgeline was covered with a heavy growth of timber except where Britton's Lane cut through. At the foot of the ridge were large fields bordered by either wormwood or better-built stake and rendered fences. It was along these fences, close to the woods, that Foster chose to form his lines. Companies B and G covered the left flank north of the lane, while the rest of the regiment formed up on the south side of the road.[7]

As Dengel brought up his guns, he deployed them at the edge of the tree line on the south side of the lane, just ahead of the Twentieth's position. He had no immediate target but was determined to get into the action. He ordered his guns to fire at a large dust cloud at the east side of the lane that, he correctly surmised, had been raised by the main body of the Confederate forces.[8]

The Missourians were taken by surprise as shrapnel suddenly rained down on them. They suffered no human casualties from the barrage, but a number of horses were slaughtered. The Missourians did not like their predicament and retreated from the field.[9] In the meadow on the Confederate right, where the Seventh Tennessee was resting, the inaccurate shelling caused some consternation when shells began to tear through the blackjack trees around them. Colonel Jackson ordered his men to mount and re-form in the woods farther to their right.[10]

The artillery barrage also had a direct effect on the Union cavalry. Watching the Missouri troopers fall back, O'Connell quickly told his men to remount and make a run for the battery. The cavalry brought with them to the Union line a swirling cloud of dust that, when added to the cannon's smoke, made an impenetrable cloud that settled on the battery.

Still, Dengel's guns blazed away at the unseen enemy until Colonel Dennis ordered him to cease fire. An eerie silence fell over the battlefield.[11]

In the Confederate lines, Armstrong sized up the situation. He now knew that he was up against a larger force, but when the small Union cavalry force scurried off toward Jackson and the battery ceased fire, he believed he had won the brief engagement. Yet, he had to be sure, and cautious.

Still blinded by the dust and smoke settling over his lines, Dennis ordered the Twelfth Illinois forward once again to see what the Confederates were doing. Meanwhile, the wagon train that Dennis had brought from Estanaula had arrived at the rear of the Union line and an urgent message had been sent to the Thirtieth Illinois to come up with all speed.[12]

The Twelfth started down from the ridgeline and advanced cautiously down Britton's Lane eastward toward the crossroads where they had first engaged the enemy. Ahead and to the left, there was a swirling dust cloud, just above the tree line. Keeping watch on this, they somehow missed the obvious, imminent danger just to their front.[13]

Suddenly, there came into view a magnificent but terrifying sight. At the end of the lane and just west of the little woods was a body of Confederate cavalry, 400 men across and three men deep.[14] The forty Union troopers, scattered across the field in a thin skirmish line, stared, mesmerized, at the force before them.

From the rebel host came the command to draw sabers. More than a thousand blades glittered in the sunlight. A Confederate officer ordered the charge, and the massed regiments surged forward toward the Union patrol. The skirmish became a race.

It was a running gun battle up to the Union lines with the Federal horsemen fleeing before the gray-clad avalanche. Finally, the Union horsemen gained the safety of the trees on the ridge. Colonel Dennis watched the charge with a growing awe and later wrote, "The earth trembled like a tornado (as) they came down on my little band of veterans . . ."[15]

Dengel's battery opened up on the Confederates as they came shouting and shooting at the Union line. Dengel's men fired cannister, then double cannister, until, just as the Southerners came within a hundred yards of the battery, the infantry opened up. The Twentieth Illinois fired a volley into the face of the onslaught, and the Confederate line crumbled as if it had hit an unseen wall. The

Union infantry, hidden among the trees, loaded and fired as fast as they could, while Dengel's men, working with the fury of demons, fired their guns, blowing huge gaps in the rebel line. In the smoke and dust, the Confederate cavalry rode over their own dead and wounded, their horses in turn tripping and falling in a tangled mass, adding to the confusion.[16]

Despite the fury of the charge, not one Confederate came within thirty yards of the Union line. This force made up of the Second Missouri, First Mississippi, and Balch's Battalion of the Third Tennessee fell back to regroup.[17] The same dust that had kept Dennis from seeing the rebels earlier had also kept the Confederates from seeing the arrival of the Twentieth Illinois on the Union line. Many Confederates thought they had been tricked and led into an ambush, which they blamed on pro-Unionist farmers in the area.

As this force fell back in confusion, another group of Southerners prepared to assault the Union left flank. On that part of the field, the Seventh Tennessee, supported by the Second Tennessee, had advanced to a point on the Steam Mill Ferry road that was opposite a large field. Their plan was to capture the Union battery.

Crossing the road, dismounted troopers kicked down the fence that bordered the field. Quickly, they formed a line of battle in the corn, their position obscured from the Federals by a slight depression in the field and the standing corn.

Several companies of the Seventh Tennessee rode forward, supported by elements of the Second Tennessee. Their charge also shook the ground, but because they were partly hidden by the corn, they were able to get much closer to the Federal battle line.

The attack fell on the two companies of the Twentieth Illinois—B and G—that had been stationed behind a high, strong, stake and rendered fence, on the north side of the lane. The inordinate height of the fence kept the rebel cavalry from riding over their position. Instead, the Union infantry, aided by O'Connell's dismounted cavalry company, kept up a deadly close-range fire that forced the Confederates to fall back.[18]

Although the Seventh's attack failed to break the Union line or capture the artillery, it succeeded in forcing Dengel's artillerymen to abandon their position. Dengel was only able to get his men back to their guns after the Confederates had gone. The Federals moved the guns back from their forward position to a point in the middle of the road where they pointed directly down Britton's Lane, a place where the gunners felt more secure.

The Twelfth Illinois Cavalry was thrown into the fight that raged along the fence on the left flank. Their job had been to protect the baggage train in the rear, but just at the moment they were called away, several companies of the Seventh Tennessee worked their way around the left flank and fell on the unprotected wagons.[19] All forty wagons were captured, along with the Union sick and wounded, the teamsters, and camp followers. The hungry Southerners looted some wagons and set eight others on fire.

Armstrong had a momentary glimpse of victory. The Federals were surrounded, and it followed that once their artillery was captured, the battle would be over. His first two mounted attacks had failed because they were not coordinated; now he wanted to take a more measured approach. He ordered the remaining companies of the Seventh Tennessee on the right flank and the First Mississippi on the left flank to charge the guns on foot, still relying on his numbers to carry the day.

The field on the south side of the lane, fronting the First Mississippi, was planted in cotton and sweet potatoes. At the corner of the field was a little farmhouse with a fenced-in garden. The distance between the Union line and the Confederate lines was about 300 yards. On the north side of Britton's Lane, the distance between the battle lines was slightly wider.

Dismounted and drawn up into one long skirmish line, the First Mississippi charged over the shattered fence bordering the fields and moved into the potato field. They were immediately met with a hail of lead fired from the Union lines hidden among the distant trees. They had hardly gone a hundred yards before the order was given to lie down. The Union field of fire was so open that the only protection the Confederates had was to lie flat on the ground.

Lieutenant J. L. Dupree of Company G crawled on his hands and knees, along with a number of his men, to the shelter of the farmhouse in the corner of the field. From this point, they tried to crawl toward the Union line along a shallow ditch that ran along the lane. Writing years afterward of his ordeal that day, Dupree noted: "From Shiloh to Selma I never witnessed a hotter fight. As proof of this my company lost a little more than two-fifths of its numbers, in killed and wounded, in less than ten minutes; perhaps in five."[20]

The attack was slightly more successful on the Confederate right flank, but only for a moment. Once again, screened by the standing corn, the men of the Seventh Tennessee were able to advance all the way to the Union line, but once again, their attack was stopped at the fence. The tall, strong fence kept the rebels from closing with their adversaries.

A desperate hand-to-hand fight ensued along the fence. Clubbing with their muskets and stabbing through the rails with their bayonets, the Federals were able to keep the Confederates at bay. With pistol and saber, the rebels fought back, but in the end it was too much for them and they fell back.

A soldier of Company E, Seventh Tennessee, later recounted the struggle along the fence:

> "The Seventh Tennessee was ordered to charge on foot through a corn field, from which the fodder had been stripped, against a heavy line of infantry lying behind a stout worm fence and in the woods. A galling fire was poured into Company E, but some of its men reached the fence. Dr. Joe Allen of Whiteville mounted the fence and fell dead on the enemy's side of it. John Bradford of Toone, and Willie Wendel, a school boy of Bolivar, were killed near the fence. D. E. Durrett of Bolivar received a wound which put him on crutches to the day of his death, which occurred a few years ago, and Tom Joyner and John Fortune were severely wounded. How so many men got out of that field alive is one of those unaccountable things that sometimes occures [sic] in war." [21]

Armstrong saw that these attacks had bogged down, so he ordered a renewed assault on the Union battery. The duty of capturing the guns fell to Wirt Adams's Cavalry Battalion, which, so far, had not been engaged during the whole campaign.

Colonel Adams formed his men in column, four abreast, on the Medon road, half a mile from the Union lines. Adams knew the only access to the guns was to ride straight up Britton's Lane directly into the mouths of the cannons.[22]

Ordering his men to draw sabers, Adams led the battalion at a walk down the Medon road. As the men advanced, the walk turned into a gallop. Then the battalion made a sharp right-angle turn into the lane as Colonel Adams ordered the buglers to sound the charge.[23]

As Adams's men turned into the lane, Dengel's guns fired a blast of double cannister. At the head of the column, Adams miraculously survived a volley that brought down three of the men beside him. With bugles blaring and men shouting, Adams could not hear or see through the dust the tragedy that had befallen his men. As each successive wave of cavalrymen passed over the dead and wounded before them, the lane became clogged with a horrible tangle of living and fallen men. The dust was so thick that those behind could not see what was going on until it was too late, when they, too, became a part of it.

Individual troopers fought their way around the congestion. Horsemen crashed through the fences lining each side of the lane in an attempt to follow their commander, who had disappeared into the battery smoke.

The sight of such wild determination was too much for the men of Dengel's battery. The gunners, sensing the cannons were about to be captured, abandoned their positions. In spite of the threats and encouragements of Lieutenant Dengel, the retreat could not be stopped. Suddenly confronted by wild-eyed Confederate troopers, the lieutenant could do little but throw up his hands and surrender, as did eleven of his men. Adams's battalion, at great cost, had captured the battery.

A trooper in Wirt Adams's command later recalled:

> "I can not forget the picture of Col. Adams as I saw him at that moment, seated on a cream colored mare, from whose nostrils the blood spurted with each heave of her panting sides, with a smoking pistol in his hand and the light of a panther in his eyes as he looked around at the dead and dying men and the few survivors who had lived to follow him through. Then he looked down the lane to where his charging squadrons were completely blocked in a confused mass of dead and wounded men and horses, realizing that there was no hope of assistance from them."[24]

Although they had captured the battery, there were too few of Adams's men to hold the ground. But now, the dismounted men of the Seventh and Second Tennessee and the First Mississippi rushed forward to the guns. Some of the angered Southerners began to beat the captured gunners with their fists, but this was soon stopped as orders were given to take the guns off the ridge. With great effort, the guns were rolled off the ridge toward the Confederate lines at the east end of the lane. Every few yards, the carcasses of horses blocked the road, impeding their progress.[25]

The Union position was in serious trouble and all but falling apart. Confederates on the Federal left flank had driven back the Union infantry by flanking their position, and everyone knew the rebels were in the rear blocking their retreat.

Sensing the crisis and knowing his men were on the verge of rout, Dennis rode among them, speaking calmly but firmly in an attempt to rally them. Later Dennis told General McClernand of the event: "At one time my men faltered and commenced falling back I asked them if they had forgotten that they were Genl MCClernand 'Old Guard' with cheers they rallied and swore they would die on the field or be victorious. They kept their pledge . . ." [26]

As Dennis strove to rally his men with speeches, his staff officer, Captain Foster, kept the more reluctant in line at pistol point. For the moment, all seemed lost, but then a dramatic event secured the Union position. The Thirtieth Illinois arrived on the scene.

Because of the heat and their exhaustion, the Thirtieth Illinois had fallen far behind on the line of march, but under the command of Major Warren Shedd, they had raced forward at the sound of the guns. Coming upon the captured baggage train, they fixed bayonets and attacked, recapturing the wagons without firing a shot. Then dressing their lines, after leaving a small guard at the baggage train, they surged forward to the aid of the embattled Twentieth.[27]

Whether taken with their temporary success or because they were too tired to see their situation tactically, the Confederates had failed to consolidate their position on the ridge after the capture of the guns. The charge of the Thirtieth Illinois hit the rebels like a runaway train. Firing as they came, the Illinois infantry drove Armstrong's men off the ridge in bitter hand-to-hand fighting, but they were too late to recapture the guns.[28]

Armstrong was dumbfounded. He had captured the Union artillery and surrounded his enemy, and now in a few moments he had seen the Federals reinforced and his command driven back to their original positions. He was where he had started over two hours before.

Even with his reinforcements, Dennis had little more than 800 men in his command. The Federals were still outnumbered three to one. His men had promised to "do or die," and it seemed it was still up to the Confederates which would happen.

Armstrong still felt he held the key to the Union position. He ordered his men to make feint attacks on the Union left flank, while he delivered a crushing blow to the Union right. He believed he knew the extent of the Union line in that sector of the field. A heavy blow on the Federal right would roll up their line and drive them off the ridge toward Denmark. Armstrong had lost a number of men, but he was convinced that victory was still within his grasp.

After the fighting of the past two hours, Colonel Dennis, like his men, was unable to see through the dust and smoke for more than a hundred yards. Dennis then took it upon himself to make a personal reconnaissance of the Southern positions. Already mounted, he spurred his horse down the ridge and through the smoke. Once beyond the haze, a quick glance told him what was in store. He saw the Confederates massing on his right flank and strong skirmish lines forming on his left.

Alarmed, Dennis rode back to the ridge to prepare his men for the new onslaught. He ordered the Twentieth Illinois to the right, or south, of Britton's Lane about a hundred yards. Then the regiment turned back on itself to form a line that resembled a giant fishhook. He then moved the Thirtieth Illinois into the position formerly held by the two companies of the Twentieth on the north side of the lane. These changes had no sooner taken place when the Confederates attacked.[29]

The quick repositioning had saved the Union line, for the rebel attack came crashing into an empty section of the woods. In the smoke and dust, unable to see clearly, many of the Confederates fired into the deserted Union position, while at the same time exposing their flank to the new Federal line.

A volley from the Twentieth Illinois brought the rebel charge to a halt. Stunned by the sudden turn of events, the Confederates broke. When a few tried to make a stand on a nearby hill, Captain Orton Frisbee of the Twentieth Illinois led a bayonet charge that drove this last detachment from their position.[30]

On the Union left, a heavy skirmish line of rebels came tearing out of the cornfield but was brought up short by the well-aimed volleys of fire from the Thirtieth Illinois. The attack there soon broke down into a confused series of sorties on the Union line.

Even as they struggled against the last heavy attack, the Union soldiers were cheered by the sight of the arrival of the Fourth Ohio Cavalry, returning from its scout toward Estanaula. Thinking these men were the advance guard of larger Federal forces, Armstrong called off his attack and left the ridge in Union hands.

The welcome sight of the Fourth Ohio meant only one thing to Dennis: his rear was clear of Confederate troops. Quietly, he ordered his men to withdraw and march toward Denmark. The wagon train led the way, followed by the artillery caissons. The infantry and one company of the Twelfth Illinois Cavalry came next, with the Fourth Ohio forming the rear guard. The badly wounded were left where they lay to become the prisoners of the Confederates.[31]

In silence, the Confederates watched the Union forces depart. Armstrong made no serious attempt to follow. After hours of fighting and hundreds of casualties, Armstrong knew he had lost. Every moment, he expected to see fresh Union troops assault him. Jackson was now out of his reach, and for all practical purposes, the raid was over. It was three o'clock in the afternoon, and Armstrong turned his troops toward Mississippi and home.

A soldier of the Third Tennessee Cavalry summed up the day in a letter to his wife: "Oh, such carnage you never saw or heard of. It is said never to have been equalled except at Donelson. Col Balch says Shiloh was nothing to compare with it. . . . Such a terrible battle I hope I may never again be in."[32]

US Army Military History Institute

Charged with guarding the railroad between Toone and Medon, Colonel Jasper Maltby found his forces spread too thin to stop Armstrong's raiders.

Reprint: Morningside Press, 1977

Robert 'Black Bob' McCulloch, the 'old school' colonel of the Second Missouri Cavalry, commanded the Confederate flanking movement at Middleburg that nearly severed the Union battle line.

Reprint: Morningside Press, 1977

West Point graduate Colonel William H. Jackson, of the Seventh Tennessee Cavalry, led the Confederate advance at Middleburg.

6

Aftermath

The Confederates were masters of the field. The first order was to gather the wounded and care for them. This was accomplished with some help from the Union prisoners because Armstrong, still fearing the arrival of fresh Union troops, kept most of his men mounted. Hundreds of wounded men, North and South, were taken to nearby farmhouses and the field hospital established by the Union forces during the battle. Both of the Federal surgeons who had been accompanying Dennis's men had been captured, and these men, doctors Christopher Goodbrake and William Freland, rendered their invaluable service to the wounded and made a favorable impression on the Southerners that lasted for years.

Hot, tired, and dusty, the Confederates were in no jubilant mood after the fight. While some tended the wounded or kept an eye on prisoners, others turned their attention to the two field guns captured from the Federals. One gun was spiked so it could not fire; the other gun, however, suffered an unusual fate. Unable to spike the second gun, the rebels tried to deny its use to the Union army by setting the gun's carriage on fire, but the carriage refused to burn. Angered, some men fell on it with axes and chopped the carriage and wheels to pieces, and in a final gesture, they took the barrel off the carriage and threw it down the well.[1]

Although they had not captured the caissons or ammunition for the guns, a number of Confederates questioned the destruction of the artillery, feeling, as many veterans later wrote, that the guns should have been taken south and turned over to the Confederate army in Mississippi.

Armstrong's command had taken more than a hundred men prisoner at Britton's Lane. Added to the others captured in the two days prior to the battle, there were now some 216 men to guard.

Armstrong stayed on the field of battle for an hour. This was all the time he allowed his men for taking care of the wounded, collecting the dead, and gathering his command together for the march south.

Avoiding the road leading to Denmark, Armstrong led his men southwest through the woods toward the river crossing at Estanaula. He laid ambushes along the roads he crossed in the belief that a large force of Union cavalry was somewhere just behind him. Late that afternoon, his harried forces camped close to the Hatchie River in front of the main Estanaula ford.[2]

Meanwhile, at Denmark, Dennis discovered the Confederates had not followed him. After waiting there for two hours, he slowly retraced his steps and soon arrived back at the Britton Lane battlefield. At Medon, Major Oliver of the Seventh Missouri Infantry, having heard the battle developing at Britton's Lane, took to the road, marching to the sound of the guns. He did not arrive at the battlefield, however, until Dennis had returned. Night was falling and the Confederates were nowhere in sight, so the two forces, Dennis's brigade and Oliver's regiment, camped on the field of battle, among the dead and dying.[3]

The next morning, September 2, the Confederates crossed the Hatchie and, after a short march, stopped at Harmony Church in Haywood County to parole the prisoners taken during the raid. Here also the Confederate host found rest. Some of the men had been in the saddle for some forty-eight hours straight, and much of that time had been spent in combat. Almost all the cavalrymen were hungry because the ten days' rations they had prepared in Mississippi had expired two days before, and Armstrong had not allowed his men to forage.[4]

By September 4, the Confederates were marching through LaGrange, having reached the raid's jumping-off point by a circuitous route. A trooper of the Seventh Tennessee later recalled: "As we passed through LaGrange (covered with dust so thick that one could hardly tell whether we were white men or black), the good ladies cheered us on our way with sweet music, both vocal and instrumental. And we needed something to cheer us up for, besides being dusty, we were weary and hungry."[5]

Now back within friendly territory, the rank and file, as well as officers, had time to reflect on the past few days and how things had developed. Another trooper in the Seventh Tennessee wrote: "We were certainly on the run, to say the least a forced march. . . . Where does the blame lie? Certainly not with the men they carried out every order and executed it as completely as the 7th (always) did."[6]

Veteran cavalryman John Milton Hubbard put the men's feelings more bluntly: "The whole command was discouraged by the operation of this raid, and felt that if we had gained anything at all, we had paid dearly for it."[7]

The fight at Britton's Lane had cast a pall over the whole operation. Yet, if the men in Armstrong's command were unsure of any advantage won on this raid, the general was not. He began by painting a glowing picture of the raid in a dispatch to his superiors. Although he admitted his men were tired and hungry, he stated, "They (his men) are ready when opportunity offers to punish the insolent invaders."[8]

Armstrong's assessment of the military situation in West Tennessee also seemed slightly askew, for in the same dispatch, he reported: "I am more firmly than ever convinced that the enemy are prepared to evacuate Bolivar whenever the advance of the army is made."[9]

It can readily be argued that the Union high command was frightened by the prospect of a Confederate advance, but not to the point of giving up their position in West Tennessee. What had

Armstrong really accomplished in this raid? Maybe, deep down, Armstrong himself had doubts about his success. Even after painting a rosy picture of the situation, the September 2 dispatch to General Sterling Price contained what could be called a disclaimer: "I have gone further probably than my instructions, but I hope my anxiety to render service and my success will be an excuse for my doing so."[10]

Armstrong, boosted by earlier newspaper reports about his victory at Middleburg, was able to present a convincing argument, at least to some, that he had indeed accomplished a lot. General Price had sent Armstrong on a reconnaissance around Corinth, but instead he had struck further north. Yet, Price seemed to have been satisfied with Armstrong. He never publicly stated that he was displeased with Armstrong for exceeding orders. Perhaps Price felt that giving Armstrong full rein of command in planning and executing the raid precluded any reservations he might have had about the results.

The Union forces felt a subdued sense of joy about their victory at Britton's Lane. The cost had been high, and even though they had concentrated more than 2,000 men at the battlefield by the next morning, they made no attempt to pursue. Dennis's force marched to Medon the day after the battle, and his men camped there for the night. The story of the fierce little fight slowly spread, and newspapers in both the North and South were seeking information.

On September 3, the Twentieth and Thirtieth Illinois Infantry regiments rode back to Jackson on a special train. Having survived an engagement against superior forces, a battle in which they expected to be wiped out, the men of both regiments were in high spirits.

Roland Evans, an officer in the Twentieth Illinois, noted this very spirit in a letter home. "It is a matter of surprise to me we were not annihilated. We are several times completely surrounded which left us either to surrender or fight our way out, we chose and carried into execution most effictively [sic] the later proposition. . . ."[11]

Another soldier with the Twentieth put it more succinctly: "The 20tieth and 30tieth feel invincible after this extraordinary victory."[12]

When the regiments arrived in Jackson, they marched in parade formation from the train station to the courthouse, where General

John Logan reviewed them. Logan, the divisional commander, had been north recruiting at the time of the battle. He addressed the troops and complimented them on their success. He was well received.[13]

General Ross and Dennis's command had saved Jackson from being raided. The battle that was supposed to have taken place at Medon had happened at Britton's Lane with the hoped-for results. The Union supply line was saved by cool reaction, desperate courage, and a bit of luck. It was one of the few times in the war that Federal troops had to face such superior numbers.

Telegraph communications between Bolivar and Jackson were restored a few days after the raid. The railroad was repaired within two weeks. The Union forces' ability to bounce back can best be illustrated by the fate of the two cannons the Confederates thought they had destroyed at Britton's Lane. By industrious effort, both guns were reclaimed and put into operating condition the day after the battle.

Although the Northern newspapers told of a stunning victory in Tennessee, not everything was rosy for the Federals. A worried Colonel Dennis wrote in a letter to General John McClernand, dated September 8, that he was discouraged and out of heart. His little brigade was now no more than a fair-sized battalion. His regiment, the Thirtieth Illinois, had only 260 men fit for duty a week after the encounter at Britton's Lane. At the same time, the Twentieth Illinois reported only 180 men present for duty.

Dennis's letter to his superior took on a begging tone. "Could I be permitted to take my Regt. to Illinois in three weeks I could have it ready for the field. . . . You see the 30th is about fought out."[14]

The request was denied. Rather, the Twentieth and her sister regiment, the Thirtieth, were allowed an extended stay in Jackson to build up their strength. There would be many more fights ahead for these men, but probably none fiercer than the four-hour stand at Britton's Lane.

The war progressed and the next big campaign came as the Confederates tried to retake Corinth. The story of Armstrong's raid and the final battle at Britton's Lane, which had occupied the front pages of every major newspaper in the North and South, was pushed from the public's view by other stirring events. The raid had begun the same day that the Second Battle of Bull Run was fought in Virginia and ended only days before the bloodbath at Antietam in Maryland. The gallantry of the men, North and South, who had fought in the first great cavalry raid in the Western Theater passed into memory.

It is uncertain just what had been gained by Armstrong in his raid or, for that matter, by the bravery of the isolated Union garrisons that opposed him. It did prove to the Union commanders that their supply lines needed to be protected. Three months later, in December, Nathan Bedford Forrest raided into West Tennessee with somewhat more success than Armstrong. By that time, however, all the garrisons along the railroad were protected by fortifications and Jackson was guarded by some 15,000 troops supported by thirty pieces of artillery.

If there were few short-range effects on strategic planning because of Armstrong's raid, there was surely one long-range effect. The nature of warfare, at least in the use of cavalry, changed. Both North and South saw what raids into the enemy rear could accomplish. If Armstrong's raid miscarried, it did presage the future.

Armstrong's raid had lasting effects, to greater and lesser extents, on all those who took part in it.

Brigadier General Frank Crawford Armstrong never rose above this rank during the entire war.[15] A month after the raid, his command was taken away and General Price gave him a staff position. It took Armstrong some time to win back the respect and confidence of his men. He would later get back his field command and distinguish himself as an officer under Nathan Bedford Forrest.

After the war, Armstrong drifted back out west and ended up an employee of the federal government. He was the United States Indian inspector from 1885 to 1889, and he was the assistant commissioner of Indian Affairs from 1893 to 1895. He spent the last years of his life in Bar Harbor, Maine, where he died in 1909. He is buried outside Washington, DC.[16]

Colonel R. A. Pinson, of the First Mississippi Cavalry, was severely wounded in action soon after the West Tennessee raid. He survived to lead his men until the end of the war. After the war, he took up the practice of law and moved to Memphis, Tennessee, where he died of yellow fever. Pinson was the first victim of the epidemic that nearly wiped out the city of Memphis in the 1870s.[17]

Wirt Adams, whose battalion was nearly destroyed while capturing the Union battery at Britton's Lane, also practiced law after the war. However, his life was cut short when John Martin, a newspaper editor with whom he had a quarrel, murdered him in 1888.[18]

Soon after the West Tennessee raid, Colonel William F. Slemons, of the Second Arkansas Cavalry, was court-martialed for, among other reasons, stealing horses from Union prisoners during Armstrong's campaign. The prosecuting officer in the case was W. H. Jackson, former colonel of the Seventh Tennessee, a newly promoted general.

It may have been inevitable that Slemons, the self-styled "wild-eyed" colonel, and Jackson, the by-the-book West Pointer, would run afoul of each other. During the trial, Jackson referred to Slemons as a "rather inferior officer,"[19] an insult that the high-strung Slemons would not let go unchallenged. In the end, Slemons was acquitted of the charges against him. He soon publicly attacked Jackson in the press, calling him a "villainous coward and scoundrel."[20] The trial and its aftermath caused the men to slip into a deep hatred of each other that lasted all their lives.

Slemons requested, and finally obtained, a transfer back to Arkansas, where he ended the war as a Union prisoner. A promotion to brigadier general came through after he was captured and thus was ruled invalid, but Slemons had a general's uniform made and was photographed wearing it. After the war, he served several terms as a US congressman, representing his home state of Arkansas.[21]

W. H. Jackson steadily rose through the ranks, informally taking the rank of major general. Although an enemy of Confederate President Jefferson Davis, his military skills proved too important to ignore. After the war, he was content to spend his life raising horses in a pastoral setting.[22]

Colonels Robert McCulloch, Charles Balch, and C. R. Barteau

proved to be competent officers during the war but passed into relative obscurity afterward. Yet, all of these men were prime movers in the Confederate veteran organizations that rose up in the postwar South.

Of the Union soldiers who at one time or another faced Armstrong during the raid, most achieved distinguished careers, both military and civilian.

Leonard Fulton Ross, the Federal general who found himself in command of all West Tennessee during Armstrong's raid, slipped back into a less conspicuous role soon after the campaign. He distinguished himself during the siege of Vicksburg, Mississippi, and when that town finally fell to Federal forces, he resigned his commission and retired to civilian life. Ross became a power in Illinois politics, both during and after the war. When asked why he had resigned his commission so early in the war, Ross stated that he knew the fall of Vicksburg was a blow from which the South could not recover. The war, he said, was all but over after Vicksburg, and time proved him right.[23]

Mortimer Leggett, the overall commander of Federal troops at Middleburg, became a key figure on General U. S. Grant's staff during the Wilderness and Appomattox campaigns. A good officer during the war, Leggett's military career did not outshine his civilian life. Leggett was a brilliant businessman who would become most noted for co-founding a little company called General Electric.[24]

Colonel Manning Force, of the Twentieth Ohio Infantry, went on to win the Congressional Medal of Honor later in the war, although he was severely wounded and disfigured for life by his act of bravery. His civilian life was built around this disfigurement. He founded a veterans organization that later became the basis for the modern-day federal Veterans Administration.[25]

Jasper Maltby, colonel of the Forty-Fifth Illinois Infantry, whose men bravely held at Toone and Medon stations, became one of the youngest generals in the Union army, aided no doubt by his friendship with General Grant. But his fame was short-lived when he, like Colonel Pinson, died of yellow fever soon after the war.[26]

Elias Dennis, the Federal commander who bravely led his men at Britton's Lane, became a valuable general officer in the Union cause. Some military historians consider Dennis the best field commander the Union army produced during the entire war. Strangely, Dennis is an unsung hero, for although he was a brilliant officer and a much-desired lecturer after the war, he died in obscurity. No contemporary newspaper of any consequence carried any mention of his passing, although he outshone many of his fellow officers.[27]

Fame for some dwindled away before the war ended.

Captain Orton Frisbie, of the Twentieth Illinois, made a name for himself at Britton's Lane by taking command of that regiment during the heat of battle.[28] Major S. D. Puterbaugh, of the Eleventh Illinois Cavalry, was praised for his keen action at Middleburg commanding the mounted reserves. Yet, both of these men were forced out of the army within two months of Armstrong's raid for neglect of duty.[29]

Lieutenant William Dengel, commander of the two-gun battery at Britton's Lane, resigned his commission a year after the fight. His depleted battery was merged with Battery A of the Second Illinois Artillery, and Dengel, passed for promotion, no longer relished field command.[30]

The hardest luck befell Private Charles Prindle, the man who claimed to have fired the first shot at Britton's Lane. He was killed in action a year later, the only original member of Company H, Twelfth Illinois Cavalry, to die of wounds during the whole war.[31]

The story of Armstrong's raid passed into local folklore in West Tennessee, and many of these legends proved over time to be untrue or exaggerated to some greater or lesser extent. But there is one story, often told and well documented, that not only sheds light on the events of the campaign but illustrates the pathos of the Civil War era.

After the battle of Britton's Lane, two local men, Bill Henry and a slave named Shedrick Pipkins, had been detailed to gather and bury the fallen Confederates. Among the bodies collected was that of a young boy, perhaps no more than fifteen years of age, who was dressed in a strangely cut uniform. For whatever reason, this unknown

Confederate struck a sympathetic chord with Mr. Henry, who reached down and cut a button from the boy's coat before filling the grave.

The button was later given to a Captain Guthrie, who carried it in his pocket during the rest of the war. Afterward, for the next twenty years, Guthrie carried the button to veterans' reunions in the hope that someone might be able to identify it and the boy who had worn it. But the button was so unusual that no one ever seemed to have seen one like it before.

It was the custom at many veterans' reunions for local people to open their homes to the old soldiers. Captain Guthrie was attending one such reunion in Atlanta when he was invited to the home of a Mrs. Jefferson, the widow of a Confederate veteran. That night, the talk around the supper table turned to the war, and Mrs. Jefferson, intently listening to the old warriors' stories, offered her own.

Mrs. Jefferson recounted how her husband had joined the Confederate army, only to be killed early in the war during the First Battle of Bull Run. Her son, Sanderson Jefferson, a boy of fourteen, burned with revenge and, against his mother's wishes, ran off to join the army. She did not see or hear from him for several months, but one day she received a letter from him in Corinth saying he had joined the cavalry. Mrs. Jefferson acquiesced to her son's service and sent him a uniform made from one her grandfather had worn as a soldier during the Revolutionary War. Sadly, she said, she never heard from her son again and was sure that he lay somewhere in an unmarked grave.

With some trepidation, Captain Guthrie produced the button from his pocket and gave it to his hostess. He explained how he came by the button. With tear-swollen eyes, Mrs. Jefferson quickly left the room. Returning a moment later, she produced not only the button Captain Guthrie had carried but also its mate, along with a piece of fabric that matched a shred that hung from Guthrie's button. For both Captain Guthrie and Mrs. Jefferson, the search was over.

On September 1, 1898, approximately 4,000 people gathered at a site near the Britton Lane battlefield to dedicate a monument to an unknown number of Confederate dead buried there in a mass grave.

This site, now part of the county park system of Madison County, Tennessee, is the oldest memorial to the men, North or South, who fought in Armstrong's raid. This monument and others more recently erected assure the sacrifice of those who gave their lives will always be honored.

US Army Military History Institute

Colonel M. M. Crocker, commanding the garrison at Bolivar, became alarmed early on the morning of August 30 after a number of reports placed a large force of rebel cavalry just outside the city.

Britton Lane Battlefield Map

A week after the battle of Britton's Lane, an unidentified officer of the Twentieth Illinois Infantry drew a map of the battlefield to accompany an account of the action that was published in a camp newspaper.

An original copy of that newspaper, with the map, is located in the Illinois State Archives. The map, however, is in such poor condition that it cannot be directly reproduced. The accompanying illustration is a copy of that map. The following description and map legend are taken directly from the original.

1. Twentieth Illinois Regiment. 2. Thirtieth Illinois Regiment. 3. Two pieces of Schwartz Battery. 4. Rebel lines. 5. Britton's Lane. 6. Main Road 7. Corn Fields. 8. Timber. t. Ravine. A. Hill and second position of Federal troops. a. Rebels preparing to charge in our rear, but our troops had out generaled them and gained their new position—result, the rebels fire without wounding a man, while our shots emptied many saddles. ++ Hospital of the Twentieth in charge of Dr. Goodbrake.

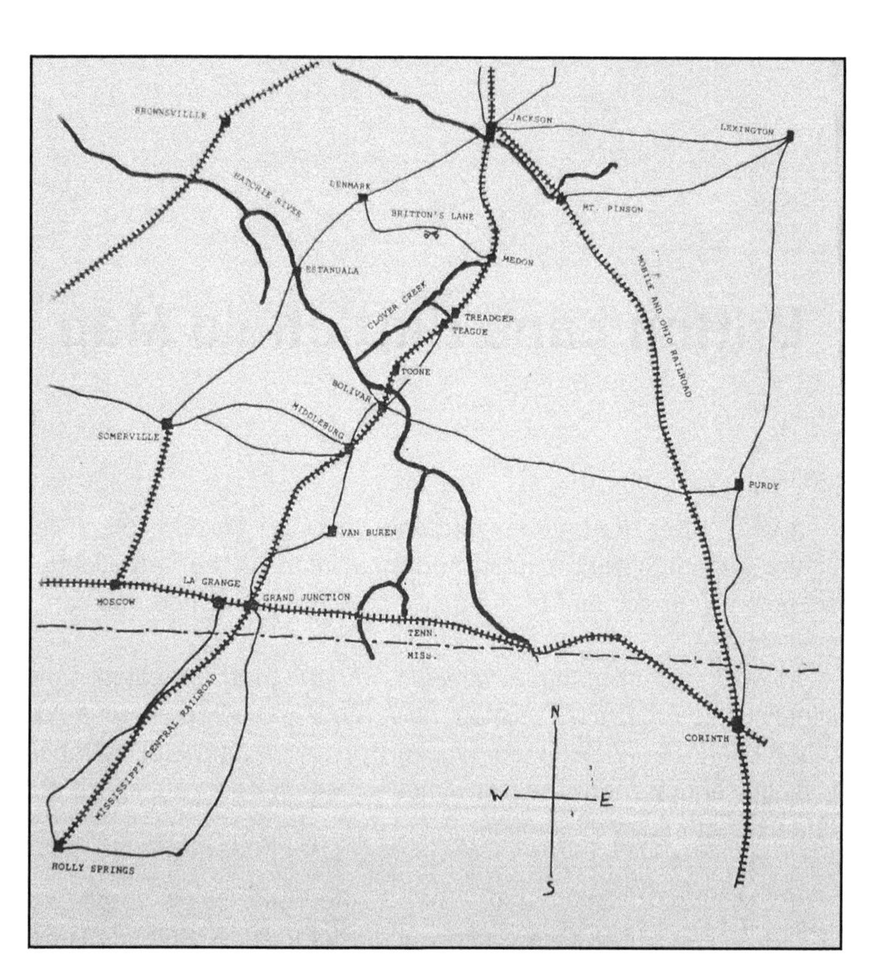
BROWNSVILLE
HATCHIE RIVER
DENMARK
JACKSON
LEXINGTON
MT. PINSON
BRITTON'S LANE
MEDON
ESTANUALA
CLOVER CREEK
TREADGER
TEAGUE
MOBILE AND OHIO RAILROAD
TOONE
BOLIVAR
MIDDLEBURG
SOMERVILLE
PURDY
VAN BUREN
LA GRANGE
GRAND JUNCTION
MOSCOW
TENN.
MISS.
MISSISSIPPI CENTRAL RAILROAD
CORINTH
N
W
E
S
HOLLY SPRINGS

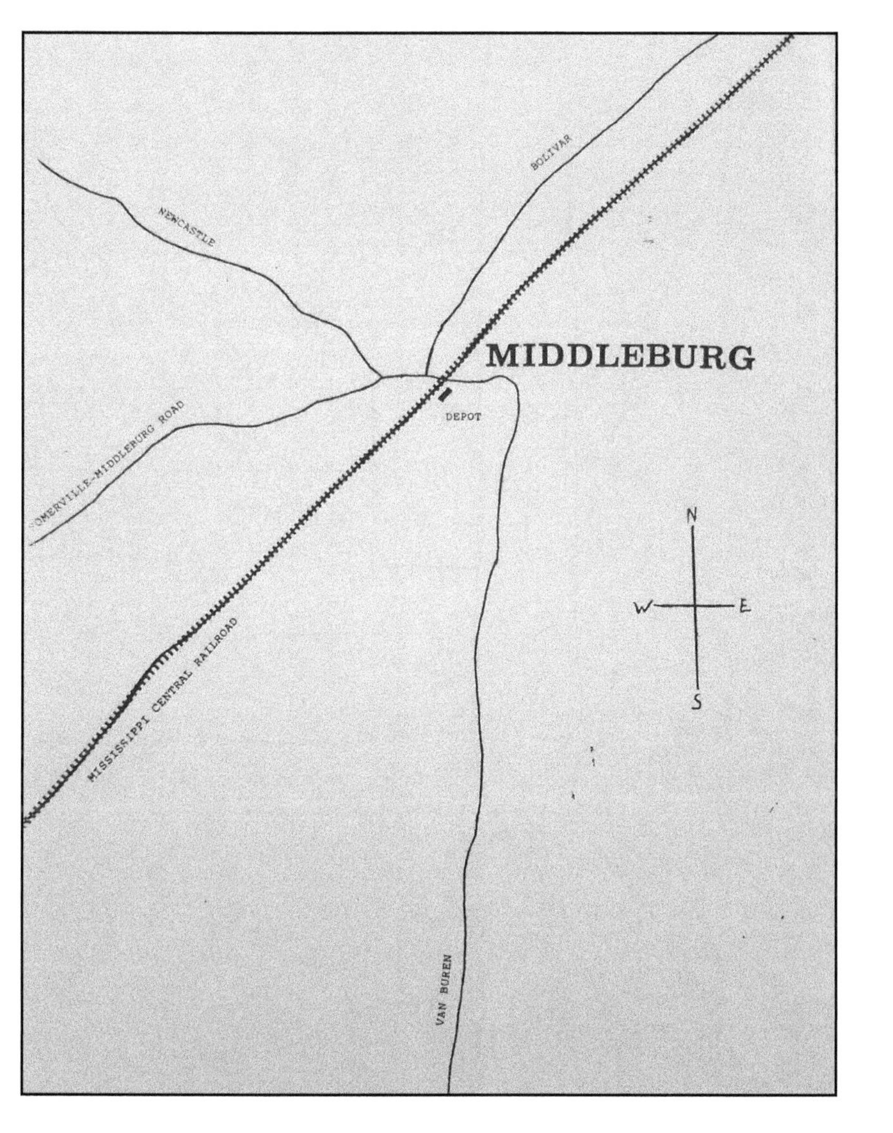
MIDDLEBURG
BOLIVAR
NEWCASTLE
DEPOT
SOMERVILLE-MIDDLEBURG ROAD
MISSISSIPPI CENTRAL RAILROAD
VAN BUREN
N
W
E
S

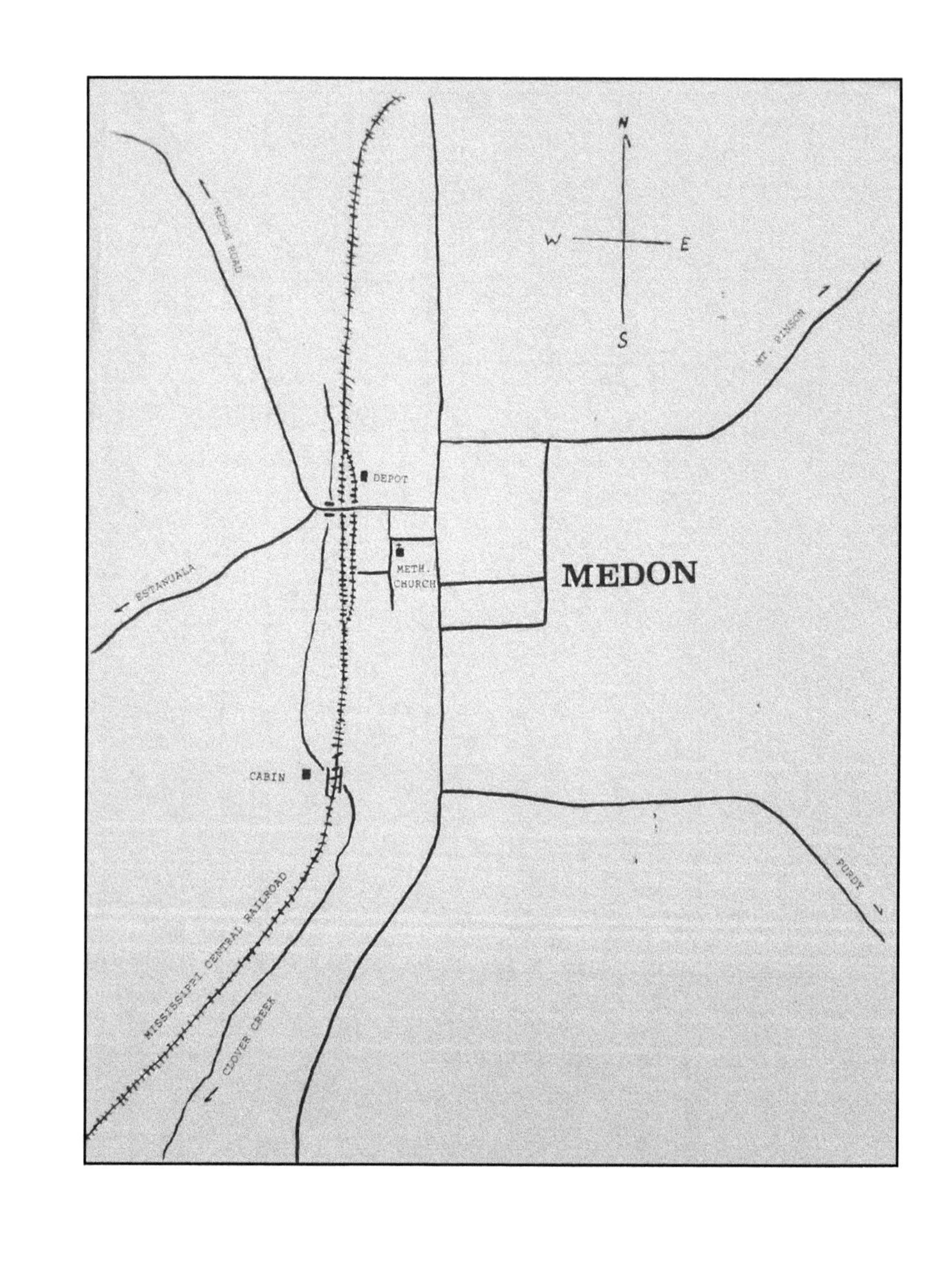
N
W
E
S
DEPOT
METH.
CHURCH
MEDON
ESTANUALA
MT. PINSON
CABIN
PURDY
MISSISSIPPI CENTRAL RAILROAD
CLOVER CREEK

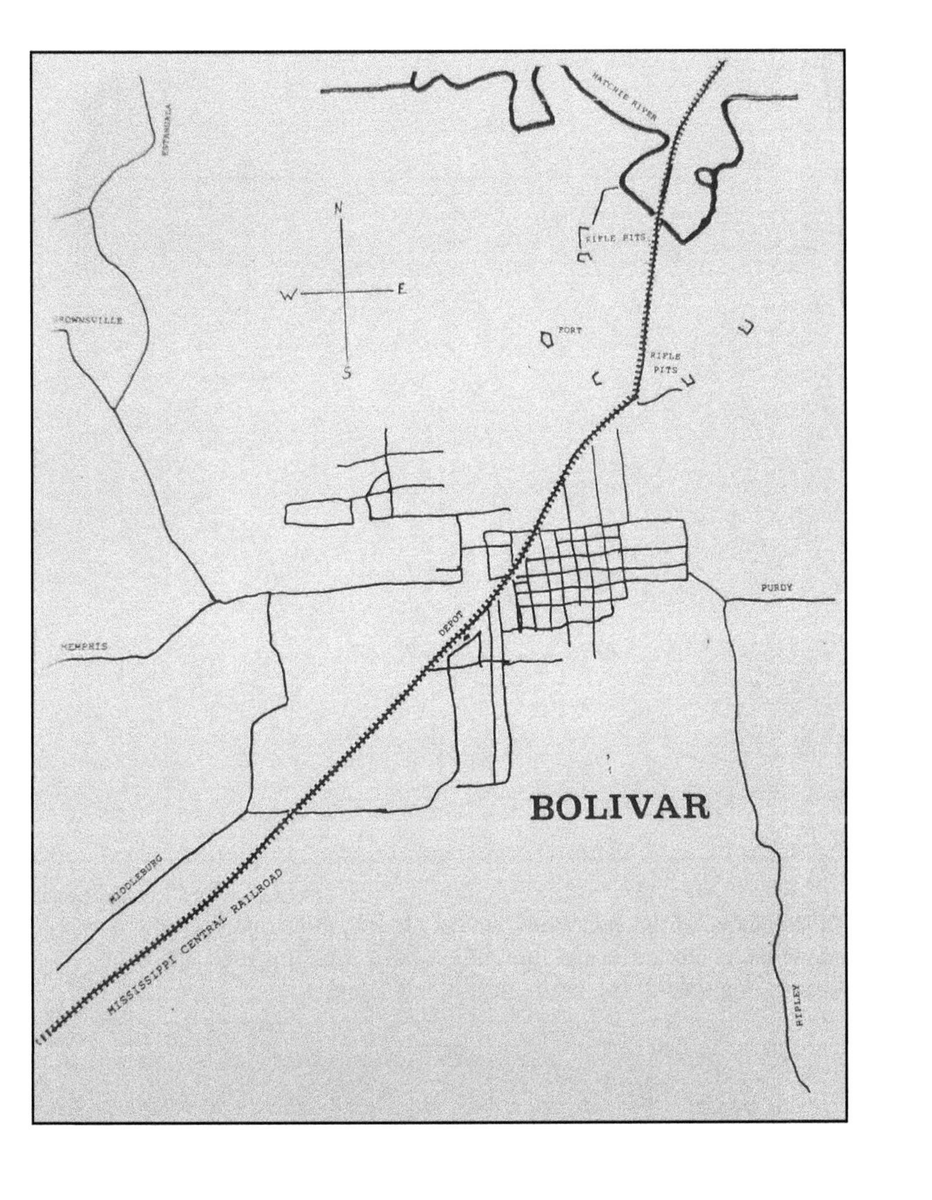

ESTANAULA
HATCHIE RIVER
N
W
E
S
RIFLE PITS
BROWNSVILLE
FORT
RIFLE PITS
PURDY
MEMPHIS
DEPOT
BOLIVAR
MIDDLEBURG
MISSISSIPPI CENTRAL RAILROAD
RIPLEY

McLean County Historical Society

Rollie Evans, of the Twentieth Illinois Infantry, drew this peaceful camp scene while stationed at Estanaula. A week later, his men would be heavily engaged at the battle of Britton's Lane.

Casualties

The figures presented in the following table represent the best account that could be gathered from available sources.

For the most part, Federal records, at least on the regimental level, were well documented. However, Confederate records were sketchy at best, so no accurate counting of their casualties can be made.

The Second Missouri Cavalry and Wirt Adams's Battalion are hardly represented in the Confederate casualty tallies, although these regiments must have had severe losses since both were heavily engaged at Middleburg and Britton's Lane. Some Confederate losses were totaled on a per battle basis and not broken down into a killed/wounded ratio. For example, the Second Arkansas recorded its losses at Britton's Lane as seventy men killed and wounded without saying how this figure should be broken down.

The official records contained casualty figures that were generally in error. Commanders on both sides seemed to have a tendency to "play up" the losses of the enemy while "playing down" their own losses. For example, Union losses at Britton's Lane were reported at 5 killed, 55 wounded, and 52 captured. But a close study of records showed that this was not the total loss, but the loss of a single Union regiment, the Twentieth Illinois Infantry, at the battle. Confederate losses were reported to be 179 killed and 100 wounded. Upon examination of the letters and reports of Union soldiers who participated in the battle, the rebel dead numbered approximately 100 with several hundred more wounded. Confederate records, though scant, seem to bear this out. The numbers of Union men captured at Britton's Lane is much more disputed, and although the Confederates claimed 213 Federals taken prisoner, a final tally of 79 captured combatants (unofficial Union tally), could be more correct. Colonel Dennis, the Union commander at Britton's Lane, writing eight days after the battle, said 125 men were captured, but this figure included teamsters and other non-combatants.

When considering losses, some note should be taken of the great numbers of horses killed in this primarily cavalry campaign. At Britton's Lane alone, more than 200 horses were killed, and many veterans, North and South, wrote in sorrow of seeing so many fine animals slaughtered.

The following table represents casualty figures based on mainly regimental records.

Casualties	Union	Confederate
Middleburg		
Killed	10	5
Wounded	18	14
Captured	71	*
Total	99	19
Treadger Station		
Killed	2	*
Wounded	1	4
Captured	40	*
Total	43	4
Medon		
Killed	5	4
Wounded	11	10
Captured	5	9
Total	21	23
Britton's Lane		
Killed	10	45
Wounded	90	114
Captured	79	*
Total	179	154
Grand total	342	270**

* Figures are incomplete or not recorded.

** Total includes the losses of the Second Arkansas Cavalry.

McLean County Historical Society

Born to a slave-owning Tennessee family, Harvey Hogg became an abolitionist and moved north. At Middleburg, he sacrificed his life and regiment, the Second Illinois Cavalry, in an attempt to save Leggett's brigade.

Appendix

The following table lists the names of men confirmed killed, wounded, or captured during Armstrong's raid. Each man is listed under the regiment in which he served. When possible, rank has also been noted.

Readers must take note that the names listed represent less than half of total casualties.

Confederate

Wirt Adams's Battalion

Company A. Killed: Lieutenant George Montgomery, Sergeant Major Lee Briscoe. Wounded: Captain A. Bondurant.

Second Tennessee Cavalry

Company A. Killed: D. Tuttle, J. P. Webb.

Company C. Wounded: Sergeant A. B. McKnight.

Company D. Wounded: Tobe Doss, William Brown. Captured: Ed Bullock, O. B. Harris.

Company E. Killed: William Joe Maddox. Wounded: William Luster, Joel Blankenship, Joe Burrow.

Second Missouri Cavalry

Company G. Killed: Sammy Massey. Wounded: Tom Turner.

Company K. Killed: Captain Rock Champion, John H. Breen. Wounded: Lieutenant Joe Eubanks.

First Mississippi Cavalry

Company A. Wounded: Lieutenant Logue, R. S. McLemore.

Company B. Killed: O. B. Canthon, J. P. Odom, ___ Lancaster. Wounded: Captain J. T. Chandler, James Barry, W. P. Reed, W. P. Howell.

Company C. Killed: J. J. Wright. Wounded: Captain Taylor, T. B. Hardy, J. W. Hare, J. M. D. Lon, J. G. Wright, S. J. Bunch, Missing: W. W. Miller, R. P. Shields.

Company D. Killed: R. J. Flannigan, Thomas T. Langham. Wounded: Alex Laughlin, S. R. Harris.

Company E. Killed: Moses Ward, J. W. Briggs. Wounded: W. E. Morrison, ___ Griffin.

Company F. Killed: Captain John R. Beale, John S. Roebuck. Wounded: Nicholas Lagrone, ___ Kerr, Nathaniel Barnett, A. J. White.

Company G. Killed. W. R. Randall. Wounded: Jacob Pierce. A. J. Lockett, F. B. Greer, W. L. Pagan, C. M. Tate, James Douglass.

Company H. Wounded: Patrick Hotton, Daniel Davis.

Company I. Killed: D. J. Hull, B. P. Sudduth, R. H. Tuner. Wounded: William C. Long, Ransom Wingo, D. A. McMurry, W. B. Dacas, Captain Turner.

Company K. Killed. Lieutenant John P. Wilson. Wounded: Lucius Harper, P. N. Howell, Thomas C. Duncan, R. N. G. Wilson.

Seventh Tennessee Cavalry

Staff officers: Wounded: Major W. L. Duckworth.

Company A. Killed: Robert W. Cox. Wounded: B. W. C. Bloydes, J. L. Henderson, E. D. Ragland, T. J. Thomas, Phil Thomas, W. R. Cox.

Company B. Killed: James Dillahunty.

Company C. Killed: Lieutenant John Albright, Ed James Carter. Wounded: Captain S. P. Bassett, Lieutenant John T. Lawler, John Stephensen, Sam Norvell. Captured: W. H. Farris.

Company D. Killed: E. S. Grove. Wounded: J. H. Reid, W. L. Anthony, R. H. Browning, Noah Leggett, William W. Tucker. Captured: J. Stephens, M. M. Frink, R. R. Groves, J. W. Sanders, W. H. Sallis.

Company E. Killed: John F. Allen, J. W. Bradford, John Breeland, Sanderson Jefferson, Ed Peters, Willie Wendel. Wounded: Sergeant J. E. Carraway, N. B. Cross, J. D. Connelly, F. Donegan, J. T. Fortune, M. Hartigan, Morris Hardrye, Thomas Joyner, J. T. Sawyer, D. E. Durrett.

Company F. Wounded: Samuel H. Young, Owen Roach. Captured: R. N. McClelland.

Company G. Killed: Samuel Dent.

Company H. Wounded: Lieutenant James Williams, John Carroll, J. B. Farmer, J. H. Stewart.

Company I. Killed: James Dunn.

Company J. Wounded: Sergeant C. C. Dodson, Joe Wray, Tom Dolson. Captured: Cyrus Bledsoe.

Company L. Wounded: James Hopper, A. L. Rainey, J. H. Robertson. Captured: W. Baxter Drake, D. C. Taliaferro.

Company M. Killed: J. M. Green, Milton Green, H. H. Hunter. Wounded: J. F. Fitzhugh.

Union

Seventh Missouri Infantry

Company A. Wounded: J. Carrick.

Fourth Ohio Cavalry (Foster's)

Killed: Sergeant John T. Smiley.

Twentieth Ohio Infantry

Company D. Killed: James Herron.

Company G. Killed: Henry H. Lockwood.

Eleventh Iowa Infantry

Company H. Killed: W. C. Budd. Wounded: Russell B. Hare, W. Hazlett, Daniel J. Parvin.

Second Illinois Artillery (Dengel's Battery)

Wounded: John Farmer. Captured: Lieutenant William Dengel.

Second Illinois Cavalry

Staff officers. Killed: Lieutenant Colonel Harvey Hogg.

Company F. Killed: Lieutenant Neil T. Shannon, Lieutenant Levi H. Lieb, Chester Elerton, William Ross, Martin W. Watson.

Eleventh Illinois Cavalry

Company C. Killed: William J. Simpson.

Company L. Killed: William Rote.

Twelfth Illinois Cavalry

Company H. Wounded: John Clark.

Twentieth Illinois Infantry

Company A. Wounded: David Waters, James McGee.

Company B. Killed: William S. Vail. Wounded: Sergeant M. L. Fanniger, August Abraham, George D. Carr, Jerome Webber, F. M. Rook, Henry Sperry.

Company C. Wounded: J. N. Brown, J. Dusch, Thomas Garrison, J. Key, David Rayburn, Jasper Hex, Jackson Davis.

Company D. Wounded: J. C. Robinson, Augustus Deedrich, George Garner, John Hartley.

Company E. Killed: James A. Stratton. Wounded: J. N. Derby, James Hall, J. McAlhaney, Reuben Gibbs, David Schmidt, J. C. Hull, John Short.

Company F. Killed: Conrad Honstine, Henry Bartlett. Wounded: Henry Shiffer, August Shearer, John Coombs.

Company G. Wounded: John Rapp, George Hanhle, Alexander Myer, Lewis LaFountain, Edwin Beuker, Henry Benschboch.

Company H. Wounded: Neals Olson, Nelson Brown, Ephraim Cassell, Charles Dixon, Joseph Mayo, Wesley Noble, John Riordan, John Roberts.

Company I. Wounded: Sergeant Thomas Jemmison, Isaac Saltmarsh, David Richardson, Aaron Hawkins, Jacob Miller.

Company K. Wounded: Martin Bissell, James Jennings, John Leach, E. Howes, Samuel Trenton, Dewitt Wilson, Greenbury Leach, George Wilson.

Thirtieth Illinois Infantry

Staff officers. Wounded: Major Warren Shedd, Adjutant Hiram Peyton, Commissary Sergeant James Allen. Captured: Surgeon William Feland, Drum Major Granville McDonald.

Company A. Wounded: Sergeant Marion Detwiler, Sergeant William Dungan, Sergeant Robert Dihel, Chauncey Smith, William Adams, John Clark, George Brown, John Gilmore. Captured: Samuel Clifford, John Cavin, William White, Samuel Dihel, Thomas Taylor.

Company B. Captured: A. C. Hammond, H. Robertson, J. H. Davenport, C. D. Kellams, Jesse Covington, W. H. Swink, J. H. Large, W. Henry, W. Barnes, W. H. Morris, H. Potter, Thomas Reed.

Company C. Captured: W. A. Brown, Spencer Taylor, Duncan Maxville, S. A. Caudle, Thomas Lunsford, J. R. Candle.

Company D. Wounded: John Montgomery. Captured: Sergeant Rufus Longnecker, Corporal John Murphy, Levi Cox, Joseph Kent, Hiram King, B. B. Longnecker, Richard Parker.

Company E. Killed: Sergeant Hugh Barker, Frederick Brenneke. Wounded: William Wetzell. Captured: Josiah McCann, Williams Miles, John Stewart.

Company F. Wounded: Andrew Runyan, James Barnett, James Quinn. Captured: Isaac Ishler, Benjamin Williams, Richard Ashmore, William Grupe, Joseph Copie, James Perry, Joseph Bramhall, Ellis Beeny.

Company G. Wounded: Sergeant William McClellan, John Garrett, William Hambert, Charles Phillips, Frank White, F. Kimmel. Captured: Lieutenant H. G. Calhoun, Captain James Burnett, John McCreight,

James Logan, William Kidwell, Lucius Personius, Patrick Malvaney, Lewis Stillman, David Willett, James Ogle, Benjamin Miller, Gillespie B. Rice, David Copeland, William Willits, James Hamilton, Reuben Gladman, Chauncey Kimmel, Aaron Patterson, Dennis Bickford, Robert Hamilton, Thomas Willett, Richard Willett, Henry K. Tyler, Samuel Boden.

Company H. Wounded: William Woods, William Holland. Captured: Daniel Chaney, Benjamin Stead, James Shaw.

Company I. Killed: John Fitzgerald. Wounded: Henry Clark, Jackson Hearter. Captured: Lieutenant Noah Reddick, Henry Gealon, Isaac Merritt, Absalom Delay, William Daniels.

Company K. Wounded: Sergeant William Johnson, Sergeant William Leonard, John Hamilton, Alfred Beetle, William Wilton, John Brennon. Captured: William Nettler, John Maddux, James M. Clarke, Daniel Hendrickson, John H. Hilbers, Frank Leigers, George Lepper, L. W. Metzger, Leander Skeen, Gavin Smiley.

Forty-Fifth Illinois Infantry

Company A. Killed: William C. Benefield. Wounded: Lieutenant David Williams, John. B. Harrison.

Company B. James Harding (missing in action, presumed killed).

Company C. Killed: Francis L. Belknap. Wounded: Peter Callahan.

Company F. Killed: Sergeant Henry Crittenden. Wounded: Captain James J. Palmer, George Shannon.

Company I. Killed: Lieutenant William L. Green, William H. Sheriff. Wounded: Sergeant James Jamieson, Orasmus Beardsley, John Jenkins.

Bibliography

Published materials

Adair, Captain John M., *Historical Sketch of the 45th Illinois Regiment*. Lanark, IL: Carroll County Gazette Print., 1869.

"Affairs in Tennessee: A Fight Near Jackson," *Waukegan Weekly Gazette* (Waukegan, IL), September 27, 1862.

Alft, E. C., *South Elgin: A History of the Village From its Origin as Clintonville*. South Elgin, IL: South Elgin Heritage Commission, 1979.

Anderson, Mary Ann, ed., *The Civil War Diary of Morgan Allen Geer*. New York: Cosmos Press, 1977.

Bailey, Durante, "Gen. Logan's Division: The Battle of Britton's Lane," *Chicago Times*, September 18, 1862.

"The Battle Near Bolivar," *Memphis Daily Appeal* (Memphis, TN), September 5, 1862.

Blanchard, Ira, *I Marched With Sherman*. San Francisco: J. D. Huff and Company, 1992.

Castel, Albert, ed., "The War Album of Henry Dwight," *Civil War Times Illustrated*, June 1980, 24–36.

"Col. Robt. McCulloch, Venerable Veteran," *Confederate Veteran Magazine*, 1905, 35.

Corliss, Carlton J., *Main Line of Mid-America—The Story of the Illinois Central*. New York: Creative Age Press, 1950.

Davis, Thomas W., *Diaries 1862–1865*, Civil War Collection. Tennessee State Archives, Nashville.

Deupree, J. G., *Confederate Veteran Magazine*, 1897, 489.

Dyer, Frederick H., *A Compendium of the War of the Rebellion*. 3 vols. Dayton, OH: Morningside Press, 1979.

Fay, Sgt. Edwin H., *This Infernal War*. Austin: University of Texas Press, 1958.

"From Cairo," *Chicago Times*, September 2, 1862.

"From Cairo: The Battle of Bolivar," *Chicago Times*, September 4, 1862.

Ford, C. Y., "Fighting With Sabers," *Confederate Veteran Magazine*, 1922, 220.

"Federal Account of the Denmark Fight," *Memphis Daily Appeal*, September 18, 1862.

"Gallantry of the ___," *Memphis Bulletin*, September 12, 1862.

Gates, John W., "Britton's Lane—Some Interesting Facts Concerning the Battlefield," *Jackson Sun* (Jackson, TN), 1897.

Gilbert, Capt., "From Capt. Gilbert's Company," *Weekly Gazette* (Elgin, IL), September 24, 1862.

Hancock, R. R., *Hancock's Diary (History of the Second Tennessee Cavalry)*. Nashville: Brandon Printing Company, 1887.

Hare, Russell B., "The Iowa Boys at Bolivar," *Muscatine Courier* (Muscatine, IA), September 15, 1862.

Holley, Donald, "Amid Showers of Shot and Shell: William F. Slemons and the Civil War," *Drew County Historical Journal* (Drew County, AR), Vol. 3, 1988, 3–16.

Hubbard, John Milton, *Notes of a Private*. Bolivar, TN: R. P. Shackelford, 1973.

Illinois. *Adjutant-General's Report of the State of Illinois*. Vols. 2, 3, 7, and 8. Springfield, 1900.

Johnson, Allen, ed., *Dictionary of American Biography*. Vol. 1. New York: Scribner, 1928.

Johnson, Robert Underwood, and Clearence Clough Buel, eds., *Battles and Leaders of the Civil War*. Vol. 2. Secaucus, NJ.

Lindsley, John Berrien, ed., *The Military Annals of Tennessee Confederate*. Spartanburg, SC: The Reprint Company, 1974.

"Letter from Adjutant Frolock," *Carroll County Weekly Mirror* (Mt. Carroll, IL), September 10, 1862.

"Letter from Captain Cowan," *Warren Independent* (Warren, IL), September 25, 1862.

"Letter from Co. G. 30th Ill.," *Keithsburg Observer* (Keithsburg, IL), September 11, 1862.

"Letter from Ichabod," *Carlyle Weekly Reveille* (Carlyle, IL), September 18, 1862.

"List of Casualties in Pinson's Regiment," *Memphis Daily Appeal*, September 8, 1862.

McCormick, David I., and Midwell Crampton Wilson, eds., *Indiana Battle Flags*. Indianapolis: Indiana Battle Flag Commission, 1929.

McDonald, Granville, *A History of the 30th Illinois Veteran Volunteer Regiment of Infantry*. Sparta, IL: Sparta News, 1916.

McNeil, E. B., "Battle of Britton's Lane," *Jackson Dispatch* (Jackson, TN), January 25, 1889.

McNeil, E. B., *Confederate Veteran Magazine*, 1903, 442–443.

Missouri. *Annual Report of the Adjutant-General of the State of Missouri*. Jefferson City: W. A. Curry, 1864.

Monaghan, Jay, ed., *The Book of the American West*. New York: Bonanza Books, 1963.

Montgomery, Franklin A., *Reminiscences of a Mississippian in Peace and War*. Cincinnati: The Robert Clarke Company Press, 1901.

Morris, "From Cairo and Thereabouts," *Chicago Times*, September 10, 1862.

Ohio. *Official Roster of the Soldiers of the State of Ohio in the War of Rebellion, 1861–1866*. Vols. 2, 6, and 11. Akron: Werner, 1891.

Powell, Col. W. H., *List of Officers of the Army of the United States*. New York: Hamersley, 1900.

Reed, W. P., "Serving with Henderson's Scouts," *Confederate Veteran Magazine*, 1929, 22–25.

Rowland, Dunbar, Vol. 1 of the *Encyclopedia of Mississippi History*, Biographical. Jackson, MS: 1916.

Rowland, Dunbar, *Military History of Mississippi 1803–1898*. Spartanburg, SC: The Reprint Company, 1978.

Sifakis, Stewart, *Who Was Who in the Civil War*. New York: Facts on File, 1988.

Speer, William S., ed., *The Encyclopedia of the New West*. Marshall, TX: The United States Biographical Publishing Company, 1881.

Stevenson, Thomas M., *History of the 78th Regiment O. V. V. I., From its "Muster-in" to its "Muster-out."* Zanesville, OH: Hugh Dunne, 1865.

Tennessee. *Tennesseans in the Civil War*. 2 vols. Nashville: Civil War Centennial Commission, 1964.

Tredup, Ralph, *South Elgin: 150 Years of Heritage*. South Elgin, IL: Crossroads Communications, 1989.

Unum, E. P., "From Jackson, Tenn.," *Chicago Tribune*, September 9, 1862.

US War Department. *The War of the Rebellion: A Compilation of the Official Records of the Union and Confederate Armies, 127 Volumes and Index*. Washington, DC, 1880–1901.

Wakelyn, Jon. L., *Biographical Dictionary of the Confederacy*. Westport, CT: Greenwood Press, 1977.

Warner, Ezra J., *Generals in Blue*. Baton Rouge: Louisiana State University Press, 1964.

Warner, Ezra J., *Generals in Gray*. Baton Rouge: Louisiana State University, Press 1964.

Witherspoon, William, *Reminiscences of '61 and '65*. In *As They Saw Forrest*. Ralph Selph Henry. Jackson, TN: McCowat-Mercer Press, 1956.

Wood, D. W., *History of the 20th O. V. V. I. Regiment*. Columbus, OH: Paul and Thrall, 1876.

Young, J. P., *A History of the Seventh Tennessee Cavalry*. Dayton, OH: Morningside Press, 1976.

Unpublished materials

Bills, John. H., Diary. Hardeman County Library, Bolivar, TN.

Biographical Sketch of William Wirt Adams. Mississippi Department of Archives and History, Jackson, MS.

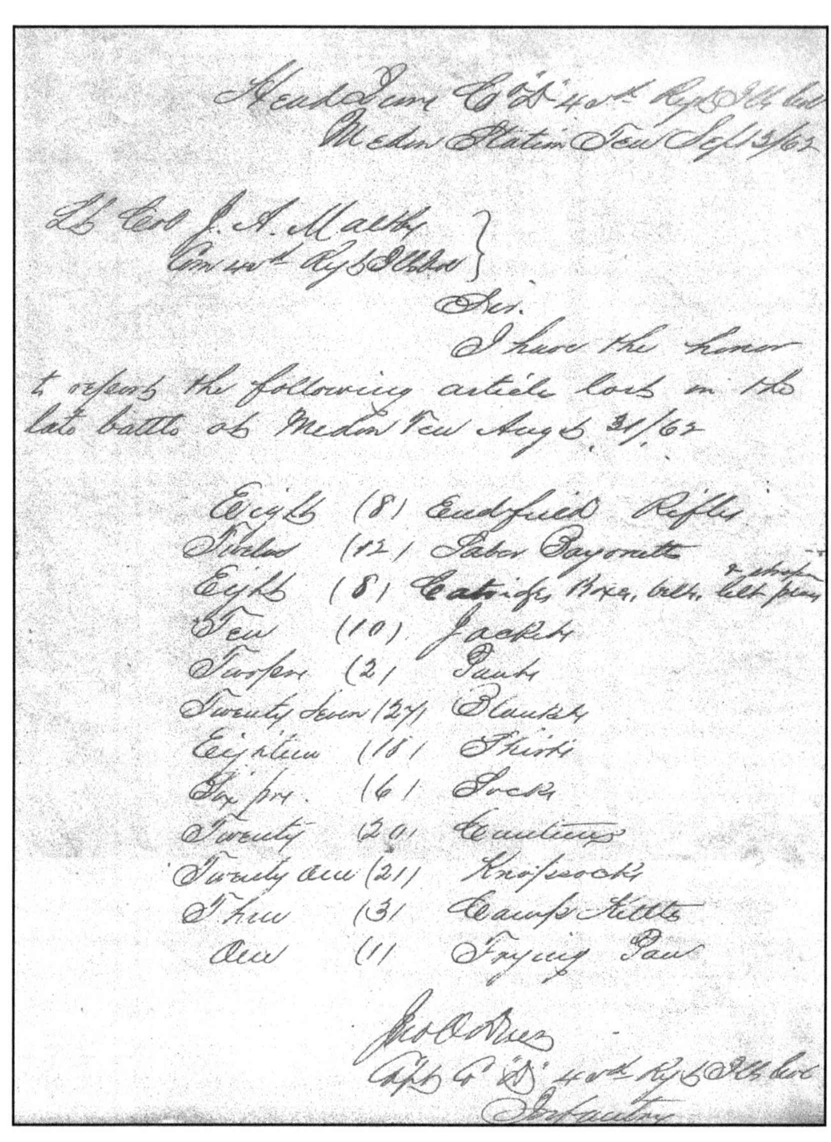

Head Quarters Co "D" 45th Regt Ill Vol Inf
Medon Station Tenn Sept 13/62

Lt Col J. A. Maltby
Com 45th Regt Ill Vols

Sir.
I have the honor to report the following article lost in the late battle at Medon Tenn Augt 31/62

Eight (8) Enfield Rifles
Twelve (12) Saber Bayonets
Eight (8) Cartridge Boxes, belts, belt plates & straps
Ten (10) Jackets
Two pair (2) Pants
Twenty seven (27) Blankets
Eighteen (18) Shirts
Six pr. (6) Socks
Twenty (20) Canteens
Twenty one (21) Knapsacks
Three (3) Camp Kettles
One (1) Frying Pan

[illegible]
Capt Co "D" 45th Regt Ill Vol Infantry

Illinois State Library and Archives

The adjutant of the Forty-Fifth Illinois Infantry lists the material losses of the regiment after the fight at Medon Station. Ill-equipped rebels seemed just as intent on capturing food and clothing as they did weapons.

Endnotes

Introductions

1. Carlton J. Corliss, *Main Line of Mid-America—The Story of the Illinois Central* (New York: Creative Age Press, 1950), 192.
2. Corliss, *Main Line of Mid-America*, 192.
3. Lew Wallace, "Letter to Susan Wallace," June 8, 1862, Indiana Historical Society, Indianapolis.
4. Wallace, "Letter to Susan Wallace," June 8, 1862.
5. Wallace, "Letter to Susan Wallace," June 8, 1862.

Chapter 1

1. US War Department, *The War of Rebellion: A Compilation of the Official Records of the Union and Confederate Armies* (Washington, DC, 1887), part II, vol. XVII, 642.
2. Ezra J. Warner, *Generals in Gray* (Baton Rouge: Louisiana State University Press, 1964), 12.
3. Warner, *Generals in Gray*, 12.
4. Warner, *Generals in Gray*, 13.
5. Warner, *Generals in Gray*, 13.

6. Allen Johnson, ed., *Dictionary of American Biography* (New York: Charles Scribner's Sons, 1928), 351.

7. Jay Monaghan, ed., *The Book of the American West* (New York: Bonanza Books, 1963), 208.

8. *Official Records*, part II, vol. XVII, 393.

9. Warner, *Generals in Gray*, 13.

10. Johnson, ed., *Dictionary of American Biography*, 351.

11. Johnson, ed., *Dictionary of American Biography*, 315.

12. Warner, *Generals in Gray*, 13.

13. Warner, *Generals in Gray*, 13.

14. Robert Underwood Johnson and Clarence Clough Buel, eds., *Battles and Leaders of the Civil War* (Secaucus, NJ), vol. 2, 725.

15. Johnson and Buel, eds., *Battles and Leaders of the Civil War*, vol. 2, 725.

16. Edwin H. Fay, *This Infernal War*, Bell Irwin Wiley, ed. (Austin: University of Texas Press, 1958), 166.

17. C. Y. Ford, "Fighting With Sabers," *Confederate Veteran Magazine*, 1922, 220.

18. William S. Speer, ed., *The Encyclopedia of the New West* (Marshall, TX: The United States Biographical Publishing Company, 1881, 246.

19. Speer, *The Encyclopedia of the New West*, 246.

20. Donald Holley, "Amid Showers of Shot and Shell: William F. Slemons and the Civil War," *Drew County Historical Society Journal* (Drew County, AR), 1988, 6.

21. "Col. Robt. McCulloch, Venerable Veteran," *Confederate Veteran Magazine*, 1905, 35.

22. Ford, "Fighting With Sabers," 220.

23. Mississippi Department of Archives and History, Biographical Sketch of William Wirt Adams (Jackson: Mississippi Department of Archives and History).

24. Mississippi Department of Archives and History, Biographical Sketch of William Wirt Adams.

25. R. R. Hancock, *Hancock's Diary (History of the Second Tennessee Cavalry)* (Nashville: Brandon Printing, 1887), 578.

26. Tennessee, *Tennesseans in the Civil War* (Nashville: Civil War Centennial Commission, 1964), 103.

27. *Official Records*, part II, vol. XVII, 649.

28. *Official Records*, part II, vol. XVII, 650.

29. Hancock, *Hancock's Diary*, 206.

30. *Official Records*, part II, vol. XVII, 662.

31. Johnson and Buel, eds., *Battles and Leaders of the Civil War*, vol. II, 728.

32. Hancock, *Hancock's Diary*, 207.

33. Hancock, *Hancock's Diary*, 207.

34. Hancock, *Hancock's Diary*, 207.

35. Tennessee, *Tennesseans in the Civil War*, 57.

36. Hancock, *Hancock's Diary*, 208.

37. Jon L. Wakelyn, *Biographical Dictionary of the Confederacy* (Westport, CT: Greenwood Press, 1977), 250.

38. Mississippi Department of Archives and History, Biographical Sketch of R. A. Pinson.

39. Dunbar Rowland, *Military History of Mississippi 1803–1898* (Spartanburg, SC: The Reprint Company, 1978), 377–378.

40. *Official Records*, part II, vol. XVII, 642.

41. Hancock, *Hancock's Diary*, 208.

42. Thomas W. Davis, *Diary 1862–1865*, Civil War Collection (Nashville: Tennessee State Archives).

43. *Official Records*, part II, vol. XVII, 687.

44. *Official Records*, part II, vol. XVII, 688.

45. Davis, *Diary 1862-1865*, 14.

46. Hancock, *Hancock's Diary*, 208.

Chapter 2

1. General Grant alluded to his fear of a Confederate re-invasion of West Tennessee in his post-war memoir.

2. Ezra Warner, *Generals in Blue* (Baton Rouge: Louisiana State University Press, 1964), 411–412.

3. Captain John M. Adair, *Historical Sketch of the 45th Illinois Regiment* (Lanark, IL: Carroll County Gazette Print., 1869).

4. *Official Records*, part II, vol. XVII, 155–156.

5. Warner, *Generals in Blue*, 118.

6. Illinois, *Adjutant-General's Report of the State of Illinois* (Springfield, 1900), vol. VIII, 722.

7. The two guns that made up Battery (Section) E were Model 1841 six-pounder field pieces. Another description of the guns mentions they were "James rifled field pieces," but this description fits only one gun, a fourteen-pounder. Still, a number of smoothbore field pieces were rifled early in the war by a method invented by General Charles T. James to improve accuracy and thus were called "James rifles." These types of altered field pieces may have made up Dengel's battery.

8. *Official Records*, part II, vol. XVII, 161.

9. Ohio, *Official Roster of the Soldiers of the State of Ohio in the War of Rebellion, 1861-1866* (Akron: Werner, 1891), vol. XII, 701.

10. Colonel Elias Dennis, "Letter to General McClernand," August 16, 1862, John McClernand Papers, Illinois State Historical Library, Springfield, IL.

11. Dennis, "Letter to General McClernand," August 16, 1862.

12. Colonel Elias Dennis, "Letter to General McClernand," August 19, 1862, John McClernand Papers, Illinois State Historical Library, Springfield, IL.

13. The Twelfth Illinois Cavalry was armed with the Second Model Burnside Carbine.

14. Adair, *Historical Sketch of the 45th Illinois Regiment*.

15. *Official Records*, part II, vol. XVII, 190.

16. *Official Records*, part II, vol. XVII, 192.

17. *Official Records*, part II, vol. XVII, 192.

18. Granville McDonald, *A History of the 30th Illinois Veteran Volunteer Regiment of Infantry* (Sparta, IL: Sparta News, 1915), 26–27.

Chapter 3

1. John H. Bills, Diary, August 30, 1862, Hardeman County Library.

2. *Official Records*, part I, vol. XVII, 46.

3. Warner, *Generals in Blue*, 102.

4. Warner, *Generals in Blue*, 279.
5. *Official Records*, part I, vol. XVII, 46.
6. *Official Records*, part I, vol. XVII, 46.
7. *Official Records*, part I, vol. XVII, 46.
8. *Official Records*, part I, vol. XVII, 46.
9. *Official Records*, part I, vol. XVII, 46.
10. *Official Records*, part I, vol. XVII, 46.
11. Illinois, *Adjutant-General's Report*, vol. VII, 527.
12. Illinois, *Adjutant-General's Report*, vol. VII, 527.
13. Illinois, *Adjutant-General's Report*, vol. VII, 527.
14. *Official Records*, part I, vol. XVII, 47.
15. J. P. Young, *A History of the Seventh Tennessee Cavalry* (Dayton, OH: Morningside Press, 1976), 45.
16. Official Records, part I, vol. XVII, 47.
17. C. Y. Ford, "Fighting With Sabers," *Confederate Veteran Magazine*, 1922, vol. XXX, 290.
18. Ford, "Fighting With Sabers," 290.
19. Thomas M. Stevenson, *History of the 78th Regiment O. V. V. I., From its "Muster-in" to its "Muster-out,"* (Zanesville, OH: Hugh Dunne, 1865), 171.
20. Stevenson, *History of the 78th Regiment O. V. V. I.*, 172.
21. Stevenson, *History of the 78th Regiment O. V. V. I.*, 172.
22. *Official Records*, part I, vol. XVII, 47.
23. Illinois, *Adjutant-General's Report*, vol. VII, 527.
24. Illinois, *Adjutant-General's Report*, vol. VII, 527.
25. Illinois, *Adjutant-General's Report*, vol. VII, 527.
26. Ford, "Fighting With Sabers," 290.
27. *Official Records*, part I, vol. XVII, 48.
28. Ford, "Fighting With Sabers," 290.
29. W. F. Slemons, "Letter to Martha Slemons," September 24, 1862, Arkansas History Commission, Little Rock, AR.
30. Slemons, "Letter to Martha Slemons," September 24, 1862.
31. Slemons, "Letter to Martha Slemons," September 24, 1862.
32. William S. Speer, ed., *The Encyclopedia of the New West* (Marshall: United States Biographical Publishing Co., 1881), 47.

33. Rollie Evans, "Letter to Mary Evans," September 5, 1862, McLean County Historical Society, Bloomington, IL.

34. *Official Records*, part I, vol. XVII, 48.

35. J. P. Young, *A History of the Seventh Tennessee Cavalry*, 45.

36. D. W. Wood, *History of the 20th O. V. V. I. Regiment* (Columbus, OH: Paul and Thrall, 1876), 18.

37. "The Battle Near Bolivar," *Memphis Daily Appeal*, September 5, 1862.

Chapter 4

1. Bills, Diary, August 30, 1862.

2. Warner, *Generals in Blue*, 412.

3. *Official Records*, part I, vol. XVII, 51.

4. *Chicago Tribune*, September 9, 1862.

5. "From Jackson, Tenn.," *Chicago Tribune*, September 9, 1862.

6. *Official Records*, part I, vol. XVII, 51.

7. Hancock, *Hancock's Diary*, 210.

8. *Chicago Tribune*, September 9, 1862.

9. John W. Gates, a Confederate veteran, noted in a *Jackson (TN) Sun* article dated August 29, 1897, that the pro-Union civilian who warned Dennis was named Henry Duncan. Unconfirmed local tradition says that Duncan was lynched by Confederate partisans in 1864.

10. McDonald, *History of the 30th Illinois Infantry*, 27–28.

11. *Official Records*, part I, vol. XVII, 50.

12. Hancock, *Hancock's Diary*, 210.

13. Adair, *Historical Sketch of the 45th Illinois Regiment*.

14. Adair, *Historical Sketch of the 45th Illinois Regiment*.

15. Luther H. Cowan, "Letter to Harriet Cowan," September 2, 1862, Galena Public Library Trust, Galena, IL.

16. Cowan, "Letter to Harriet Cowan," September 2, 1862.

17. *Chicago Tribune*, September 9, 1862.

18. *Chicago Tribune*, September 9, 1862.

19. *Chicago Tribune*, September 9, 1862.

20. Russell B. Hare, "The Iowa Boys in Bolivar," *Muscatine Courier* (Muscatine, IA), September 15, 1862.

21. Hare, "Iowa Boys in Bolivar," September 15, 1862.
22. Hare, "Iowa Boys in Bolivar," September 15, 1862.
23. Fay, *This Infernal War*, 148.
24. Hancock, *Hancock's Diary*, 211.
25. John Milton Hubbard, *Notes of a Private* (Bolivar: R. P. Shackelford, 1973), 33–34.
26. Mary Ann Andersen, ed., *Civil War Diary of Morgan Allen Geer* (New York: Cosmos Press, 1977), 51.
27. Missouri, *Annual Report of the Adjutant-General of the State of Missouri* (Jefferson City: W. A. Curry, 1864), 247.
28. *Chicago Times*, September 10, 1862.
29. *Official Records*, part I, vol. XVII, 50.
30. Cowan, "Letter to Harriet Cowan," September 2, 1862.
31. Hubbard, *Notes of a Private*, 34.
32. "The Battle of Britton's Lane," *Chicago Times*, September 13, 1862.

Chapter 5

1. *Chicago Times*, September 13, 1862.
2. *Chicago Times*, September 13, 1862.
3. "From Capt. Gilbert's Company," *Weekly Gazette* (Elgin, IL), September 24, 1862.
4. *Weekly Gazette*, September 24, 1862.
5. A number of Confederate veterans of Britton's Lane noted the "suddenness" with which the skirmish developed. Many accounts noted the casualness with which the skirmish line was first viewed.
6. *Chicago Times*, September 13, 1862.
7. *Chicago Times*, September 13, 1862.
8. *Chicago Times*, September 13, 1862.
9. Ford, "Fighting With Sabers," 290.
10. William Witherspoon, *Reminiscences of '61 and '65*, in *As They Saw Forrest*, ed. Robert Selph Henry (Jackson: McCowat-Mercer Press, 1956), 88.
11. *Chicago Times*, September 13, 1862.
12. *Chicago Times*, September 13, 1862.

13. *Chicago Times*, September 13, 1862.

14. *Chicago Times*, September 13, 1862.

15. Elias Dennis, "Letter to General McClernand," September 8, 1862, John McClernand Papers, Illinois State Historical Library, Springfield, IL.

16. *Chicago Times*, September 13, 1862.

17. Fay, *This Infernal War*, 150.

18. "Gallantry of the ___," *Memphis Bulletin*, September 12, 1862.

19. "From Capt. Gilbert's Company," September 24, 1862.

20. John W. Gates, "Britton Lane—Some Interesting Facts Concerning the Battleground," *Jackson Sun* (Jackson, TN), August 29, 1897.

21. Hubbard, *Notes of a Private*, 35.

22. E. B. McNeil, *Confederate Veteran Magazine*, vol. XI, 1903, 442.

23. McNeil, *Confederate Veteran Magazine*, vol. XI, 442.

24. McNeil, *Confederate Veteran Magazine*, vol. XI, 443.

25. Hancock, *Hancock's Diary*, 212.

26. Elias Dennis, "Letter to General McClernand," September 8, 1862.

27. McDonald, *History of the 30th Illinois Infantry*, 28.

28. McDonald, *History of the 30th Illinois Infantry*, 28.

29. *Chicago Times*, September 13, 1862.

30. *Chicago Times*, September 13, 1862.

31. *Chicago Times*, September 13, 1862.

32. Fay, *This Infernal War*, 150–151.

Chapter 6

1. Witherspoon, *Reminiscences of '61 and '65*, 90.

2. Hancock, *Hancock's Diary*, 213.

3. Missouri, *Annual Report of the Adjutant-General of the State of Missouri*, 247.

4. Hancock, *Hancock's Diary*, 214.

5. Hancock, *Hancock's Diary*, 214.

6. Witherspoon, *Reminiscences of '61 and '65*, 91.
7. Hubbard, *Notes of a Private*, 35.
8. *Official Records*, part I, vol. XVII, 52.
9. *Official Records*, part I, vol. XVII, 52.
10. *Official Records*, part I, vol. XVII, 52.
11. Cowan, "Letter to Harriet Cowan," September 2, 1862.
12. Andersen, *Civil War Diary of Morgan Allen Geer*, 52.
13. *Chicago Times*, September 13, 1862.
14. Dennis, "Letter to General McClernand," September 8, 1862.
15. Warner, *Generals in Gray*, 13.
16. Warner, *Generals in Gray*, 13.
17. Mississippi Department of Archives and History, Biographical Sketch of R. A. Pinson.
18. Mississippi Department of Archives and History, Biographical Sketch of William Wirt Adams.
19. Holley, "Amid Showers of Shot and Shell," 7.
20. Holley, "Amid Showers of Shot and Shell," 7.
21. Speer, *The Encyclopedia of the New West*, 247.
22. Warner, *Generals in Gray*, 153.
23. Warner, *Generals in Blue*, 412.
24. Warner, *Generals in Blue*, 279.
25. Warner, *Generals in Blue*, 150–151.
26. Warner, *Generals in Blue*, 309.
27. Warner, *Generals in Blue*, 118–119.
28. *Chicago Times*, September 13, 1862.
29. Both of these men's service records appear in the *Illinois Adjutant-General's Report* listed under their regimental rolls.
30. Illinois, *Illinois Adjutant-General's Report*, vol. VIII, 722.
31. E. C. Alft, *South Elgin: A History of the Village from its Origin as Clintonville* (South Elgin, IL: South Elgin Heritage Commission, 1979), 12.

Order of Battle

Confederate

Brigadier General Frank Crawford Armstrong
(Escort Company: Company E, Sixth Tennessee Cavalry)

Armstrong's Brigade

Second Arkansas Cavalry: Colonel W. F. Slemons
Second Missouri Cavalry: Colonel Robert McCulloch
Second Tennessee Cavalry: Major George Morton
Wirt Adams's Cavalry Battalion: Colonel Wirt Adams
Third Tennessee Cavalry (one battalion): Major C. Balch

Jackson's Brigade

Seventh Tennessee Cavalry: Colonel W. H. Jackson
First Mississippi Cavalry: Colonel Robert A. Pinson

Union

Brigadier General Leonard Fulton Ross

At Middleburg:

Colonel Mortimer Leggett commanding
Twentieth Ohio Infantry: Colonel Manning Force
Seventy-Eighth Ohio Infantry: Colonel M. Leggett
Second Illinois Cavalry: Lieutenant Colonel Harvey Hogg (killed)
Eleventh Illinois Cavalry (two companies): Major S. D. Puterbaugh
Ninth Illinois Light Artillery (one section): Lieutenant William Hight

Between Toone and Medon:

Forty-Fifth Illinois Infantry: Colonel Jasper Maltby
Eleventh Iowa Infantry (one company): Captain Ben Beach
Seventh Missouri Infantry: Colonel W. S. Oliver

At Britton's Lane:

Colonel Elias Dennis commanding
Twentieth Illinois Infantry: Captain Orton Frisbie
Thirtieth Illinois Infantry: Major Warren Shedd (wounded)
Twelfth Illinois Cavalry (one company): Lieutenant C. O. Connell
Fourth Ohio Independent Cavalry Company: Captain Charles Foster
Second Illinois Light Artillery (one section): Lieutenant W. Dengel (captured)

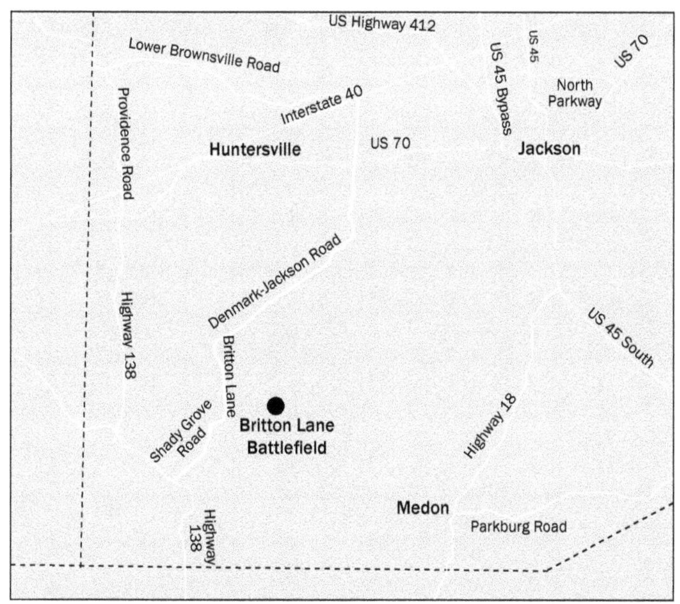

Britton Lane Battlefield

On September 1, 1862, Confederate Colonel William H. Jackson's Seventh Tennessee Cavalry, Forrest's brigade, attacked the Twentieth and Thirtieth US Infantry, Cavalry, and Artillery under the command of Colonel Dennis, near Jackson, Tennessee. The Battle of Britton Lane resulted in the capture of a large Union wagon train, two pieces of artillery, and 213 prisoners. Monuments mark the site, along with a mass grave of Confederates killed in the action. An extant cabin on the site was used as a Federal and Confederate hospital. After the battle, eighty-seven Union soldiers were imprisoned in the Denmark Presbyterian Church near Britton Lane Battlefield. The structure still contains graffiti left by the Union prisoners.

Britton Lane Battlefield is located at 4707 Steam Mill Ferry Road, Medon, TN, 38356. For more information, visit www.madisoncountytn.gov/Facilities/Facility/Details/Britton-Lane-Battlefield-1

Some proceeds from this book will go toward the preservation and maintenance of Britton Lane Battlefield.

www.ingramcontent.com/pod-product-compliance
Ingram Content Group UK Ltd.
Pitfield, Milton Keynes, MK11 3LW, UK
UKHW020140250726
13967UKWH00002B/781